Amazing
Intuition

Expanding Your Most Important Resource

Debra
Busemeyer
Baker

Copyright © Debra Busemeyer Baker
Cover photo and logo © Debra Busemeyer Baker
Cover photo design Ryan T. Dale
Copy editor Julie Hess
Proofreaders Tamara Underiner and Beth Talbert
Interior design Ryan T. Dale

ISBN: 978-1-62646-911-2

Published by BookLocker.com, Inc., Bradenton, Florida.

This book is not intended, nor should it be used, as a substitute for the medical advice of physicians, mental health practitioners or other health care professionals. The reader should regularly consult a health care professional or physician in matters relating to his/her health and particularly with respect to any symptoms that may require diagnosis or medical attention.

In order to maintain the anonymity of my clients, I have changed the names of individuals and places as well as identifying characteristics and details.

Printed in the United States of America on acid-free paper.

BookLocker.com, Inc.
2014

First Edition

To my Dad,
Donald Busemeyer

Love you forever

Don —
Thank-you for your
love and support.

Nadine

Contents

Introduction
Before We Embark

As a professional psychic since 1989, my experiences have been consistently compelling and uniquely riveting --nothing short of amazing. It is my hope that this book offers you some of the tools and wisdom I have developed during this time as well as perhaps entertains you. Psychic development – all of life, in fact – can be fun! I hope that you enjoy reading this and applying the principles as much as I enjoyed writing it. And, I have to confess. Before writing it, I did require a push.

The Nudge

A few years ago following the late Christmas Eve service at church, I had this time-stopping sense of my own mortality. It had been a sentimental, very sweet and spiritual service. Now please understand – Christmas is my nirvana. I *love* it! It comprises all things that bring me joy – family, gifts, decorations, music, lights – multidimensional celebration! At this point in the evening things were winding down. I was looking around at my husband and children gathering up their coats and belongings when the moment happened. Looking at these people whom I hold most dear, the thought stopped me in my tracks, "I will not be having this human life forever. There will be holidays in their future that will not include me."

At first I wondered if I were having a premonition of something that might soon happen, but after consideration, dismissed the idea. Then I pondered, what would I want to leave behind after I am gone? What evidence will there be that I once walked the earth -- and had the incredible experiences that I have had? I have done much inner exploration into spiritual matters, talked to many, many beings on the "other side," and have a unique perspective of the human experience. Interestingly, the beliefs of my family members range from deeply spiritual to barely accepting the idea of a higher power, some quite different from my own. Even as we sat in church marking this special occasion, I could tell that some of them were there just because I had asked them to be. My certainty of the Universal Life Force moving in, through, and as us has been key to the joy and meaning I know as I go about my daily round. This certainty, while planted in my earliest days, grew to fruition as it has been proven repeatedly through my spiritual work and exploration. I believe what I see and know to be true.

What I realized is that I wanted to write it down in case someone might want to know what I have learned.

That was the inspiration for this book. That, and so many of you have asked me to put in writing what I have been teaching in classes and seminars about how to tap into and expand your intuition. Many of my clients, as I'm sure many of you my readers as well, would like to be able to do what I do – give psychic readings, predict the future, see into people's hearts and souls, do healing energy work, observe past lives, get the occasional glimpse of God and the very frequent conversation with spirit guides and guardian angels. Or you may just be looking to tune in more easily to your own inner wisdom, perhaps help yourself and your loved ones find direction and purpose to your days.

I had a vision recently of my deceased father's memorial service where I could see his spirit watching over us. Dad looked about the church and into the heart of each person, which he could easily see in his out-of-body state. Then he came to me with tears in his eyes. "They are all so wonderful!" he seemed to be saying. "Wow! I didn't know." Now that he could understand each one fully, he could see our pure hearts and loving motivations. Not that he had ever questioned them before. But he didn't expect so many to come to his service and *to care about him so deeply!* Not only that, but he recommitted himself to supporting us all with his unconditional love from the place in Spirit that he now occupies. What my dad saw in my vision was similar to what I see when I do readings and energy work for my clients.

Each of us is a vulnerable soul, tender and sweet at our very core. Years of earth experience have formed various layers of our personalities, some which seem to support us, others that feel as though they suck the very life from us. When we come to see in our truest selves that we are spirit, pure and One with God, we come to understand how wonderful we are. Truly.

I have heard in countless sessions with clients while I channeled (communicated with) their loved ones who had passed away, "If only you could see how beautiful you are, how wonderful, how precious." They see us in our totality – the human personality we have adopted during this human experience, the huge dance of energy (auric field) around us, the dreams in our hearts, and especially the secrets we keep – and they cannot find words to describe just how exquisitely it all fits together to make the beautiful beings that we are.

My deepest motivation is to help people. If I can, by offering this book to you, make your life a little easier, a bit more joyful, and maybe even more fun, I will be satisfied. Having looked into the hearts and souls of so many people since 1988, I singularly believe that people are intrinsically good.

Our Journey Together

Just as you do a lot of preparation before you actually set forth on a journey, so too will this book include some "prep work." Chances are, your reading this book indicates that you have been interested in developing your intuition for some time and you may have even wondered why it hasn't happened as you might like. In chapters 1 and 2, we will look at some of the common obstacles most people face before allowing themselves to tune in to the information that has been there all along. In fact, some of the techniques might help you through other challenges in your life as well.

The middle chapters get to the heart of things – just *how* do you do it? The first time I was asked to teach a class on this subject, I had to sit down, sort through my psychic tool box, analyze my own techniques, and figure out my process – similar to when my little brother took apart the toaster to see how it worked. I realized that while some people describe a single 'sixth sense,' I see it as several additional senses. I introduce them to you and help you to home in on them. Just as people tend to have stronger abilities in some senses than others (like my friend who can hear me whisper from across the room!), so too do people tend to have varying abilities in experiencing their psychic senses. Once you figure out what your strengths are, you can build on them and learn to trust them.

The rest of the book seeks to answer the questions I am most commonly asked that include:

- How did you get into this line of work?
- Have you always been psychic?
- How do I help my intuitive children?
- Do you see ghosts?
- Have you ever seen a ghost who was an animal?
- How do you *know?*
- What's the difference between a spirit guide and an angel?
- Why can't I tell that my deceased loved ones are around me?
- How does your practice work?
- What is karma?
- What are chakras?
- What do you mean by energy work?
- What is Reiki?
- Why do I have to meditate?

The Exercises

At the end of each chapter is a series of questions for you to ponder. These workbook pages provide you the opportunity to apply the concepts presented to your own experiences. I suggest that you take the time to answer the questions as a gift to yourself. You don't need to share it with anyone and there won't be a grade. (No one will even check your spelling!) In fact, for most of the questions there is no "right" answer, so you can feel free to express whatever you need or want.

Some of your responses will change as you go through your life, so you may want to revisit them in a year or so to see how you have changed.

Once You've Finished

It is my intention that after reading my book you will have a deeper knowledge of yourself, your talents and abilities, and, most importantly, a greatly increased sense of just how precious you are and how blessed we all are to be having these human experiences we call lives.

While there is much more about the world that we don't understand than that we do, the link between the knowing and the unknowing is where all possibilities lie. When we let go of what we know in search of what is being revealed, we are in that moment of potential...the magical space between leaving the diving board and cleanly slicing into the water. **The power is in the letting go**.

My English teacher spoke of 'willing suspension of disbelief.' I suggest you set aside what you have known and create a space for a new understanding to enter. I suspect that what you will find has less to do with intuition and more to do with inspiration.

It is my privilege to share this journey with you. Thank you for giving time to exploring the ideas in this book, and for buying copies for your friends and loved ones. I hope you look upon it as a little love letter from my soul to yours.

1
Overcoming Obstacles

Everyone has intuition. It is crucial to our well-being. Cave men and women relied on it for survival. So forget the question, "Do I have *the gift?*" Yes, you do! Just like you have the gift to see the beauty in a sunset or hear the joy in a baby's laughter. Your intuitive or psychic abilities are stronger in some areas than others, just as some people have great athletic ability while others are master musicians.

While a few rare individuals are born with the ability to use their intuitive skills fully, the rest of us require a bit of preparation. When I look back on my development, I was preparing for this work for several years before I started using my psychic skills. My father valued psychic ability and somehow saw it in me. He used the ESP testing cards with me when I was young, and I vaguely remember being surprisingly accurate. I was at once intrigued and afraid of such "paranormal" things. It wasn't until I was a young adult that I became specifically aware of my gifts and my willingness to explore them.

Regardless of where you might be in your spiritual journey, there are likely some obstacles to your experiencing the level of intuition you seek.

So what might stand in the way? Hmmmm... Let's consider. Fear? A sense of unworthiness? Doubt? Frustration? Maybe all of the above?

7

Let's take a closer look...

Fear

There are usually two types of fear that surface while people are preparing to open up their psychic abilities. Fear of evil. Fear of inability. Sometimes we experience both.

1. Fear of Evil

In my case, I had to overcome the fear that I might tap into something horrible or evil that would harm my loved ones or me. Even though reassured by Sis, the psychic who first told me that I had "the gift," I still needed to go through a process that was ultimately just a test of my faith – do I believe in a Higher Power? And will that Higher Power, whom I usually call God, keep my family and me safe? Will God, maybe through angels and spirit guides, help me along the way?

I pondered these considerations seriously and at length -- sometimes feeling certain I was safe, and other times holding my breath hoping that something awful would not happen. Ultimately I had to face my fears -- look them squarely in the eye and see what they were hiding. I developed a technique that I use to this day. I ask, "What am I afraid of?" The first answer is usually the surface fear. Once I've explored my initial fear, I ask again and again, going a little deeper each time.

I used this technique once with my daughter who was throwing up because she was so fearful about something at school. Our conversation started with an I-don't-want-to-go-to-school theme and evolved into, "I'm afraid."

"So what are you afraid of?" I asked gently.

"That my friend is mad at me."

After talking about the subject of their disagreement, I asked again. This time the answer was, "I'm afraid I don't have any friends."

"And what would that mean?" I pursued. I rephrased the question a few more times until she got to the underlying reason.

"That I would be alone." There it was. The root of her fear. And, I would argue, the root of many if not most of our fears. Being alone, unprotected, vulnerable. Naming the root of her fear was the turning point.

For me, the fear search took a slightly different course. In a quiet moment, I asked myself, "What am I afraid of? What is scaring me?" At the time I believed that there was in the world a source of evil (the devil) and I was afraid it was out to get me. I wrangled with this idea for quite some time. If there were something out there lying in wait for my weakest moment, what could I do about it? I was living by the Golden Rule, trying to be a good person. I did not deliberately try to hurt anyone. In short, I was doing the best I could. So, I reasoned, if Evil were out to get me, there was nothing I could do about it, which only added to my fear.

The process of facing fear can intensify before clarity and peace surface. The stakes were high, though, so I persevered. 'Something' was out to get me and there was nothing I could do about it. I felt totally alone in this process, given a gift that could destroy my family and me.

I was afraid that by using my intuition to help people, I could hurt my family. There, I allowed myself to think the unthinkable. My "gift" could be the undoing of all I held sacred.

Or could it? (On the other side of my brain a little voice was laughing at me, "Get a grip. Aren't you letting your imagination run rampant?") Yet I knew this fear was the crux of it. I could stay paralyzed by fear or move through it. Fear is, after all, just an emotion. And this kind of fear is about being powerless. I had no control over the outcome. What if, despite my best efforts, I ended up hurting someone? Recognizing my powerlessness did not assuage my fear.

What Made the Difference

Two things that happened at this point helped to free me. I "worked the steps" and I had a conversation with my spiritual director.

I applied the principles of the first three of the 12 Steps (originally of Alcoholics Anonymous, but now used by many recovery-oriented groups). I admitted I was powerless --over evil, whether it existed and if it were out to get me; over the fear, over the outcome, all of it. I already believed in God, so I "came to believe" that this Higher Power just might "restore me to sanity" or at least help me get past my immobilizing fear. And then came the first turning point, the third step. I realized that while I am powerless, God is not. Perhaps this Infinite Being would take care of me. Looking at my other option (remaining in fear), I grabbed at this life raft with both hands.

Mentally and emotionally, I began "turning it over," basically praying about everything. And things got better. The old axiom that faith edges out fear proved itself to me.

Ultimately, the "letting go, letting God" part formed the basis of all of my spiritual work. I am powerless when someone comes in for a reading and asks me a question. It is not up to me whether or not the question is answered, or to what degree, or even whether the answer I intuit is accurate. So I let go and trust. Not because I am some spiritual guru but because I have no other option.

The second event, the conversation with Greg, my spiritual director, provided me with another tenet that I use to this day. I was worried that being psychic would put me at odds with the religion in which I had been raised. Greg counseled me to keep God at the heart of things, focus on the positive, which we agreed I had already been doing. Finally he said, "Do you want to know what the Church's official stance is on things of this nature?" Of course!

The church does not have a blanket criterion for all things paranormal, he said, but prefers to take things on a case-by-case basis. Its stance: *"Wait and see what kind of fruit it bears, and then judge it accordingly."* So instead of prejudging anything, the church waits to see what happens. Wow! What a relief. While I could not believe that a God I expected to be good and all-loving would judge me unfavorably for using gifts I had been given to help others, it was a relief to learn that the church that I held so dear would not judge me either, at least not without waiting to see the outcome of my efforts.

So fear of evil was conquered, at least for the moment. But what about fear that you cannot access your intuition?

2. Fear of Inability

Again, the same fear-facing technique will help, especially if there is something deeper hiding beneath, "I'm afraid I can't." Probably underneath the layers is a fear of looking foolish. None of us want to feel embarrassed. So, surround yourself with supportive, honest, loving people. In fact, I'd recommend that anyway! Your inner voice can be critical enough. You do not need those around you being critical as well.

Quite often however, your fear of inability is a cleverly disguised sense of unworthiness.

Unworthiness

A counselor I knew once said, *"There are things you believe and things you know."* So while you might believe that you are worthy of being psychic or using the gifts that you have, do you truly *know* that you are? Most of us have an entire collection of insecurities which we can recite a whole lot more easily than articulating our positive traits.

So here's a challenge for you. In a quiet moment, write down all the things that make you *believe* that you don't deserve to get what you want. Get as honest as you dare. Imagine trying to beat your worst critic to the punch. Your list might look something like this:

Why I Don't Deserve the Good Stuff

1. My car is dirty
2. Impatience with my kids
3. Gossiping
4. Skip church on Sundays
5. Fat thighs
6. I'm not perfect

Then take a moment to get real. Imagine you are living your last day on earth. Will any of that really matter? Who cares besides you? *Can any of these things actually block your good?*

You don't have to be perfect to accomplish anything. So let go of the perfectionism and let yourself try something new. Repeat after me, "It's not my first mistake and it won't be my last. It's not the end of the world." When my children were young, I even found myself saying it to them, "Yeah, Mommy made a mistake. It's not the first time and it won't be the last, so get used to it!" And then we'd laugh. Really, I was saying it to myself, and because I wanted to model for them that it was OK to make mistakes and they didn't have to be perfect. *Allowing yourself to make mistakes might be the most freeing thing you ever do for yourself.*

The cool thing about talents is that you don't have to earn them. They are already yours. And you can't lose them either. My sister goes months without playing the piano, but when she sits down at the keyboard, she plays as if she practices daily. Similarly, there is no unwritten contract about your intuition, that you have to use it or lose it, or that you have to solve murders or find missing persons to be able to keep it. You can use it as simply as finding your car keys or a good parking space.

One caveat. For me, and I stress this is my experience, if I try to use my psychic ability to "show off" or impress someone, it often does not work. I believe that I have developed my talents to help people. I take it pretty seriously and try to keep my ego in check. It seems my ego can block my tuning in ability.

I think it helps to have a sense of humor throughout the process and approach it playfully at times. Once when I was watching the World Series with my husband, I knew what every pitch was going to be before the pitcher released it. "Ball," I'd say seconds before it left the pitcher's hand and the umpire called it. "Strike." "Strike." After a while I lost interest and stopped when I saw that my husband's joy at watching the game was diminishing and I was getting a little bored. However it did illustrate for me that everyday life presents countless opportunities to test our intuition.

My favorite example while I'm on this subject happened when I was in 7th grade. It was after school and I was talking to one of my classmates who had a quarter. He tossed it in the air and said, "Call it."

"Heads," I *knew*.

"You're right," he said and smiled. "Do it again." Again I was right. After 23 more times (we started counting shortly after we started), we got bored with it. Then his bus was called so we stopped. We both laughed about it as he left.

So you've conquered your fear and feel that you deserve this, but it's still not happening...

Doubt

Of course you doubt. This intuition business is likely outside your comfort zone. So what to do about it? My friend Bob used to say to me almost weekly, *"What you focus on increases. If you focus on the problem, the problem increases. If you focus on the solution, the solution increases."* So if you focus on your doubt, "this will never work," guess what. It probably won't.

When I was a little girl, my siblings and I were not allowed to say the word "can't." We weren't allowed to give up without even trying. My children can say the same thing. A defeatist attitude does not serve you.

So you doubt. OK. No harm in a little healthy skepticism. I invite you to prove to yourself that using the techniques in this book will expand your intuition. You just might surprise yourself.

One of my favorite stories is about the man taking one of my classes who was working as a school janitor. While he said he doubted that he had any ability -- even though there he was in the Expanding Your Amazing Intuition class -- his intuition proved to be astonishing. We had partners in the class and did mini-readings for one another. Since there were an uneven number of people in the class, he became my partner. The first thing he said was, "I knew I would be your partner before I sat down." He proceeded to tell me things over the next two weeks that were, well, amazing. He saw that my son was being cyber-bullied, that my daughter would get her degree in art education, and on and on. Not everything he said was accurate. No one has 100% accuracy. What was fun were the unusual things he picked up on. He even "saw" my grandmother with details down to the bouquet of lilacs she was holding. You guessed it – lilacs always remind me of her.

It's OK to be a "doubting Thomas" -- just don't let it get in the way of your fun and exploration.

Frustration

So... you keep trying and trying with no 'luck.' A couple of thoughts:

1. Are you really trying and trying or did you give up after just a few efforts?

   Like anything worthwhile, the results increase with the efforts. So keep trying, varying the technique each time until you find the one that works for you.

2. How are you measuring your results?

   You'll see later on that there are many ways for Spirit to speak to us, and it's up to us to learn the language of Spirit.

In chapter 5, we will take a deeper look into frustration and other emotions along with their effect on our lives and our intuitive ability. Meanwhile, acknowledge the frustration when it arises but don't allow it to get in the way of expanding your amazing intuition!

In a Nutshell

Congratulations! You have embarked on a wonderful journey. As you look over your shoulder one last time to make sure you brought everything you need, do a quick mental check. So far you have or are about to:

✓ Examine your own fears, both the fear of evil (if you have it) and the fear of inability
✓ Kick your sense of unworthiness to the curb
✓ Work through your self-doubt
✓ Pack away your frustration
✓ Complete the exercises

The exercises that follow each chapter are meant to guide you into further exploration. The more honest you allow yourself to be as you complete them, the more benefit you will derive from the process. Remember, no one needs to see your answers.

I've seen plenty of people who want things to happen *their way.* "I want to hear voices." Or, "I want to see the future." Just as we aren't conscious of choosing our talents, such as that knack you have for making perfect mashed potatoes, we don't remember that conversation we had with Spirit just before we were born where we agreed upon our strengths and shortcomings for this go-round. What might have happened if Tiger Woods decided to go into swimming? He was fortunate to uncover his talent at a young age and develop it to its fullest. As you proceed through this book, you will learn whether you're a psychic golfer or swimmer, or maybe a pole-vaulter or a runner.

Chapter One Exercises

1.What are you afraid of regarding your incredible, untapped intuition?

_____

_____

What is under the surface of that fear?

_____

_____

What is under the surface of that fear?

_____

_____

(Keep asking that question until you feel that you have reached the *root fear*.)

2.What might happen if you were suddenly able to access your psychic ability at will?

_____

_____

What about that ability scares you?

_____

_____

3. Why I *Think* I Don't Deserve the Good Stuff
   a) _____
   b) _____
   c) _____

4. A Quick Three-Step Check-In

Step One: Over what are you powerless?

_____

_____

_____

(Hint: Everything *other than* your own thoughts, feelings, and actions)

Step Two: Do you believe that a "power greater than yourself" could provide you what you need?

_____

_____

What are the alternatives either way?

_____

_____

_____

Step Three: Are you willing to let go (of control, of fear, of doubt) and "let God?"

_____

_____

_____

What might it look like if a force stepped in and helped you?

_____

_____

Allowing yourself to make mistakes might be the most freeing thing you ever do for yourself.

2
Gearing Up

Maybe, just maybe, this might work for you. Now that you're ready to tune in, here are some practical tips to help set the stage. Briefly, ask for Spirit's help, trust yourself, let go of any confusion you might have, and surround yourself with supportive people.

Put the White Light Around You – Ask for Spirit's Help

This practice is not just for when you want to "be psychic." It works all the time, and I recommend that you use it daily.

Visualize the brightest, most brilliant, white light you have ever seen. Some people call it the White Light of Christ, or the Light of the Christ. It really doesn't matter what you call it or what your religious beliefs are. This White Light is pure energy, powerful and protective. It is the personification of Source, God. Take a moment right now and picture it. If you concentrate on it a little while, you will begin to feel its calming presence, its peace.

Now imagine the White Light totally surrounding you, so that nothing can touch you without going through the White Light first.

   o   Some people like the idea of an eggshell. While an egg shell protects the vulnerable little chick inside, it still allows in light and air and everything that the baby bird needs. So the light/shield won't keep out anything that you need, but it will block any energy that doesn't serve you.

o   Another image might be a White Light plastic bag with a seal-able top. I personally don't like this one because it brings to mind thoughts of suffocation, but your imagination might allow for a breathable plastic bag!

o   My favorite is to picture a White Light energy force, a two- to three-foot wide field of light, all around me that is impenetrable by anything that is not aligned with my own best interests. It will allow in love and peace (and chocolate), and keep out negativity (and excess calories ~ although I'm still working on the calorie part).

Some of this invites you to explore your own spiritual beliefs. Does your version of God include Divine Protection? If so, you might not feel the need to ask for it. However, even if you feel that you are constantly protected, I think calling upon the White Light creates an affirmation, speaks a prayer. "God / Source / Universal Life Force, I know you are with me now."

I can feel you asking, "Just what am I being protected *from?*" While I believe in a benevolent universe that is conspiring for our highest good, I also acknowledge that there are sometimes discordant energies out there. Affirming the White Light calls forth only the energies and messages that will support, empower, and help us. Have you ever noticed that people who expect only the best usually get it? This exercise puts you in that category. If there are various levels of information that you can access, don't you deserve the very best? Yes, you do.

Putting the White Light around someone or something is really a form of prayer, and I practice it nightly. When I was a little girl, my dad taught us a bedtime prayer that went like this: "Please bless Mommy and Daddy, (siblings), grandmas and grandpas, aunts and uncles (and we had plenty!), cousins (plenty of those too!), friends and enemies." I still do a version of that prayer except that now I picture each loved one and see them surrounded in Light. If someone is anticipating a challenge such as a test or surgery, I visualize them going through it amidst the White Light with ease and grace, happy and successful.

A White Light example...

When I first started using my psychic abilities, my children were quite young and my husband traveled on business Monday through Friday every week. Which meant I was home alone a lot and outnumbered three-to-one! I would lie awake at night and worry that if something happened, like a fire, would I be able to rescue all three of them, whose bedrooms were on two different floors of the house. So I visualized the White Light surrounding each of my children and me, and the entire house. I imagined that my house was invulnerable to potential intruders or anything that would harm us in any way. (Note to young parents: the White Light did not keep out nightmares of the flying monkeys after I naively allowed my children to watch The Wizard of Oz one night.)

Picturing the White Light became a habit and I routinely affirmed it around the children, the house, the car, the yard, the preschool, wherever we were. I still get chills when I think of the vivid demonstration we experienced of how well it works.

One summer afternoon, I uncharacteristically set up the kids' wading pool on the patio rather than in the yard, where I normally put it. Our patio was directly out the back door of our wood-shingle-sided home, and the gas grill was in the corner between the wooden lattice fence of the patio and the house. For dinner that evening, I had decided to try my hand at grilling some fish fillets and was told to preheat the grill for 20 minutes first. While the grill was preheating, I was inside preparing the rest of the meal. My oldest daughter, who was 4, came inside and said, "Mommy, we have a fire."

"I know, Honey," I told her. "Mommy's heating the grill."

"No, Mommy," she persisted, "we have a FIRE!"

I rushed outside to find the grill engulfed in flames. I could see the flames licking the sides and overhang of the wooden house, and my first instinct was to grab my children and rush to the neighbor's house to call the fire department. But upon closer inspection I could see that the house was not catching fire. A voice spoke inside my head, "Put the fire out yourself."

I looked around to see if I could find a bucket or water toy in the pool, which was right in front of the grill. There was not a toy in sight, so I stepped into the pool and began to splash at the flames. When I had them decreased somewhat, I reached into the blaze with my hand, turned off the gas, and then continued to douse the rest of the flames.

Adrenaline pumping, I surveyed the situation. There was not one sign that there had been a fire at all. The house and fence were not singed. My hand and arm were not burned. The only evidence left behind was the hose dangling from the gas tank. Apparently, the hose had been twisted so that it pushed on the bottom of the grill. When the grill got hot, the hose melted and the gas, instead of going inside, escaped out of the hose beneath it, engulfing it in fire.

As I look back on it, I know the White Light kept the house from catching fire, kept me from getting burned, and kept my children safe inside the house until it was all over. I wonder if having my hand wet, since there were no toys in the pool, protected my skin from burning.

Trust Yourself

Sure, it's easy for me to say, but trusting yourself is the basis not only for allowing intuition a voice in your days, but truly for a happy life. Think about it. Going around plagued with self-doubt robs you of your joy. That's not to say that all of us don't have moments of uncertainty; it's more about the percentage of time it is allowed to occupy your thoughts. *"Progress not perfection."* If you feel that you are unsure 90 percent of the time, try to drop it to 85. Little by little you can whittle away at it.

If right now you cannot believe yourself, then please believe me. You and the Creator are One. I have been hearing this message directly from my Spirit Guides and yours since 1988, and I have no reason to doubt it. *You have inside of you greatness beyond your wildest dreams.* I have seen it, and so have you. Glimpses of glory.

Moments of miracles. A force that you can harness to get what you want.

A word about getting what you want

Forget what you learned at the dinner table when you didn't want to eat your peas, and your parents told you about the starving children of (insert name of third world country). Your "waste" does not deprive someone else, nor does your wanting good things in life. Repeat after me,
There is plenty to go around.
There is no shame in your desire for good things for yourself and your loved ones. The universe is infinite and abundant, and your having something does not deprive someone else of it.

And be careful, because that tricky inner saboteur may have convinced you by now that *wanting* things is OK, but getting them is a whole other matter. Notice if you find yourself saying, "Someday I'll have beachfront property / prosperity / a happy marriage." *Someday never comes.* Beware of postponing your happiness by thinking of it in future terms. No need to postpone the day your ship comes in. There is plenty of room in the harbor today.

Again it gets back to the focus of your thoughts. Remember, "What you focus on increases." So focus on allowing the messages to come to you. Focus on receiving *lots* of messages. Focus on knowing just what they mean. Focus on being able to help yourself and others with your newfound wisdom. Focus on all the good that will result from your letting go of your doubts. Focus on what a blessing you are to yourself and others.

Letting Go of Confusion—You Might Be Wondering...

1. "Is there really information available to me?"

Before you can begin to tap into the Source of all information, it helps to accept, or at least be open to learning, that what you need to know will become available to you *when you need it.* Stop and think about it a while, and you will be able to come up with many examples of when you needed to know something and the answer just popped into your head. Divine guidance is constantly seeking us out.

> *If you believe that we are all connected in Spirit / God / Universal Life Force, then it is easy to realize that a magical collective energy is teeming beneath the surface of your consciousness awaiting to be tapped for Divine Inspiration.*

Let's say you wonder which grocery store has good corn on the cob right now? Very quickly, the answer comes to mind and you go there. Not only do they have it, but also it's the best corn you've ever tasted. OR, you go there and they don't have corn on the cob, but you run into your best friend from high school and have a wonderful visit. In both situations, Spirit is guiding your experience.

Once while traveling, we had to stop "too soon" at a rest area, not 30 minutes after starting our trip. "Didn't you go before you left?" I lamented, and then told myself that this line of questioning was not helpful. A few minutes after we were back on the road, we came upon a horrific traffic accident that I feel certain would have involved us if "someone" had not had to use the restroom. Spirit looks out for us.

One of my favorite affirmations is, *"I always know what I need to know, when I need to know it."* This is Truth for everyone. When I have a client scheduled for a psychic reading, I don't need to know until we are sitting down what information Spirit would like me to relay to them.

Which brings up the next question:

2. "What if my question is not answered?"

The affirmation says, *"What I need to know,"* and let's face it, we don't always know what's good for us. Oh, we think we know. But we don't always.

In my personal life, I was given advance notice when both of my parents were getting ready to die, even though in my mother's case her disease (emphysema) did not appear to be advancing very quickly, and in my father's case, he had not yet become ill. Yet when another family member was dying, I was not given advance warning.

There are some things we are supposed to know, and some things that are none of our business... until they are our business.

Once a friend wanted some direction about which house to choose when she and her family relocated cross-country. Try as I might, I could not bring to mind a single detail about either house. I accessed other information, but nothing about the houses. "I'm sorry," I told her, "I just don't see them." She thanked me for what I had to offer and called several days later to say that the job offer had fallen through.

"No wonder you could not see either house!" she told me. "Neither one was truly an option." Sometimes no answer *is* an answer.

3. "What if I get the wrong answer?"

Do not be discouraged. No one is right all the time, even those people who think they are ~ or maybe especially those people!

Actually there are two answers to this question:
1. Sometimes the answers are incorrect. Human error, perhaps? Inaccurate interpretation?
2. Sometimes the answers are incorrect and yet they move us in the direction we need to be going.

There is value in every answer that we get, so do not be quick to dismiss an answer because it appears incorrect on the surface. For example, you're doing some psychic play with someone and they say, "What color car do you see me driving?"

You see the color blue in your mind's eye and tell them. "Nope, it's white," they respond, summarily dismissing your intuition. However, the next week they buy a blue car. You were seeing into their future. Or maybe their last car was blue. So it's helpful to keep a collection of information to use for comparison purposes, maybe jotted down in a small notebook or kept in the notes section of your smart phone or computer.

Say your friend asks you if the guy she just met is "the one." Your intuition tells you that he is not and you relay the message. Once your friend lets go of the expectation that he is the man of her dreams, she relaxes and allows the relationship to develop in a more peaceful manner. Ultimately, she discovers that he is the man she wants to marry and tells you that your intuition was wrong. However, you can see that the information she received from you allowed her to relax and not put undue pressure on the relationship, which allowed it to blossom in its own time frame. While the information appeared wrong, the result was that she moved in the manner she needed.

4. How do I know the messages are 'real'?

There is no simple answer to this question, except to trust your instincts. And your instincts are what you are questioning. So how *do* you know when it is Spirit talking and when it is your imagination?

First of all, it is easy to confuse the two because they can be the same thing. Spirit can talk to you through your imagination. Think about it. Where does your imagination come from?

One time I pictured a vehicle that I wanted. It had all the options, was the top-of-the-line model. A few years later it was sitting in my garage. So did I foresee it? Was it a coincidence? Did I manifest it? More importantly, does it matter?

As the saying the goes, the proof of the pudding is in the eating. So see how your answers bear out. Try not to put too much at stake when you're starting out. I find it very helpful to set the answers aside and look at them later.

This is especially true when I do automatic writing for myself. When Spirit is talking through us, to us, the most striking thing about it is that it seems so *normal!* Because it has been happening your whole life, you just haven't paid that much attention before. Whenever you sit down to write a letter or anything that requires some thought, you are offering Spirit the opportunity to help you. The main difference between writing a thoughtful thank-you note and doing automatic writing is the content.

For example, you might wonder how to express to your friend just how much it brightened your day when she sent you those flowers. The God-essence in you reaches out through your words to touch the God-essence in her, creating a true Namaste moment, clearly divine. Another time you decide to sit down and journal. As you ponder, "I wonder what is mine to do in this situation," you find the answers coming to you in wave after wave of inspiration. Again, Spirit communicating through you.

I invite you to allow the inspiration to flow out through your words with others as well as in your inner dialogue. Talk kindly to yourself and create relationships with people who also speak kindly to you. Which brings us to the last part of our chapter...

Surround Yourself with Supportive People

By now you may have noticed a recurring theme... this information is helpful not only to open up your intuition but *also to open up your happiness.* Being surrounded by a circle of support is good for us! Having our own cheering section helps us learn about ourselves, believe in ourselves, feel more content, and less alone. It's kind of like waking each morning to the same forecast, "Sunny and warm."

Of course, everyone has their bad days, so again we're looking at percentages. Seek out those, and be one of those people, who are more of an 80-percent-happy than a 20-percent. You can spot them; it's easy. When it rains, they say, "Thank you God for the free water for my garden today!" And they are not Pollyannas either. They still bring the umbrella, and they share it with you. They ask you how you are, and they wait for you to answer. They make time for you in their lives with no hidden agendas. It seems like your happiness is as important to them as their own, and *this is crucial...* they give you the space to define it for yourself.

Unsupportive people are inevitable in our lives. Pretty often we're related to them. Sometimes we even marry them. That doesn't mean they are bad people. Sometimes we can look in the mirror and find a naysayer. Yikes! *Remember: you can change yourself; you cannot change other people.* So don't waste your energy trying to change someone else's percentages. If they want to be happy only 20 percent of the time, they have that right. You might find that as you become more focused on the positive, some of that just might rub off on those around you. The rub-off seems to be inversely proportional to how much you want them to change, however. Recognize your powerlessness over others and honor their right to be as unhappy as they want to be. Just don't pitch a tent in their Campground of Negativity!

When my mother way dying of emphysema, I caught her smoking on the sly. She knew she was killing herself and I could tell she felt horrible about it. Instead of trying to make her feel worse, I validated her right to choose. "You have the right to do whatever you want to do," I told her. "I still love you." Somehow I knew that she needed my unconditional love a whole lot more than a lecture on the hazards of smoking. Also, I realized that my words were not going to make her quit.

So how do you find supportive people?

Chances are, they are already in your life. At one point in my life, I became aware that a lot of my friendships felt like one-way streets. The one way involved my giving and their receiving. I decided to see what I could do about it and, no great surprise, I found that *I* was a lot more responsible than I wanted to believe. I discussed it with my friend, Jenifer, and she asked me straight out if I considered her a "taker." I was taken aback by her forthrightness because my thoughts had been leaning in that direction. She pointed out to me numerous occasions when I set it up so that I was the giver, leaving little room for her to give back to me.

"Hmmm," I reflected, "maybe I like being the giver. Maybe it seems more noble." Unconsciously I had been setting it up so that I had the upper hand in the giving / receiving arena. I see this a lot with my clients. People think "it is more blessed to give than receive" means that "it is inferior to receive" and they *undermine* the natural flow of a relationship. Before you cast someone out of your life because they are unsupportive, be open to the possibility that maybe the two of you can create a mutually beneficial friendship that blesses both of you.

It is extremely powerful to accept someone exactly as they are. I have a friend who is very loud, which can be embarrassing when you're with her in public. I love her, though, and accept this flaw and don't expect to change it. She has so many other wonderful qualities.

Psychic Partners

Try looking around at those you call your friends and see if any of them might be willing to walk the journey with you as you develop your intuition. You might be surprised to find willingness in unexpected places. I would suggest you enlist just one or two people. It is actually helpful if you do not know them very well so that there are more things you can uncover with your psychic abilities. Here is a brief list of what you need from your Psychic Partner:

1. Positive attitude
2. No right-or-wrong mentality
3. Open mindedness
4. Sense of humor

You may have been surprised that I recommend a sense of humor, but I believe that being light-hearted and fun helps others along the way. I once had a client, Julie, who was trying to figure out which of two guys she was dating was better suited for her. When I tuned in, all I saw was a tube of toothpaste, which I hesitatingly told her. She laughed and laughed. When she finally caught her breath she said, "That is hilarious! The one guy is always brushing his teeth while talking to me on the phone!" I shared the chuckle.

When I teach this in a class, I pair up the students with someone else in the class that they don't know. At first they are hesitant, but it only takes about 30 seconds to get beyond it. It is uncanny the 'random' partnerships that are formed, and the similarities are noted from the get-go. My 'scientific' assignment goes something like this: "We have 12 people in the class, so starting with you, count off 1, 2, 3... When we get to 6, start over at 1. OK, now the 1's get together, and the 2's and so on."

While I was driving to teach on the first night that I used this method, I had a conversation with Spirit about how to form the pairs to ensure that students would gain the most from the class. By the time I reached the church where the class was held, I had my method in mind, but didn't tell anyone. It was fascinating to watch as students selected one chair and then moved to another, as though guided by unseen hands.

If you do not have the benefit of taking a class, enlist a friend to read the book and go through the exercises with you.

In a Nutshell

You're getting on your way now with developing your Amazing Intuition, putting the White Light around yourself, not only when seeking information from the Divine, but all the time. As you develop your trust in yourself and your blossoming abilities, some of the confusion is likely slipping away. You may now realize that there actually is information available to you. As you develop your discernment, you may find yourself able to accept that sometimes you don't get answers to the questions you ask, sometimes the answers appear to be wrong, and sometimes they are wrong. It's not an exact science!

You will learn, as you work through the process, to differentiate which messages are the most helpful and seem the most real, and to choose carefully your support system. At the risk of sounding like a scratched CD and repeating myself yet again, it really helps to surround yourself with supportive people. When you find someone who agrees to bolster your confidence as a neophyte psychic, you will find it rewarding for both of you.

Chapter Two Exercises

1. Do the White Light exercise and picture the "brightest, whitest, most pure light you can imagine completely surrounding you." Choose an imagery that feels comfortable to you. What does it feel like?

_____

_____

Picture it around your car, your home, and your loved ones. *Practice this every morning.*

2. What is your self-trust percentage? How much do you trust...

- when something feels right?
- when something feels wrong?
- that someone is telling you the truth?
- that someone is lying to you?
- that you need to rethink it?

- that the timing is right?
- that the timing is wrong?
- that you are making the right decision?
- your own motions?
- someone else's feelings?

Assigning 10% to each question, what is your percentage? This is completely unscientific, designed only to help you examine *how much you pay attention to your inner voice.*

3. Explore for yourself: Do I believe it is OK to want things for myself or my loved ones?

_____

_____

Do I truly believe I deserve to get what I want?

_____

_____

4. List things that you want (nothing is too frivolous; no one has to see this list)

_____

_____

_____

_____

_____

5. Name some friends, acquaintances, or family members who might be willing to help you explore your intuitive abilities. Ask one or two of them to give it a try.

_____

_____

_____

3
Tuning In

Picking up psychic messages is a lot like receiving radio signals. If you have one of those old radios where you turn the dial to tune in the stations, you can probably relate. One day your favorite station comes in perfectly clearly, the next it's a little fuzzy. Two days later, you have to move the dial to get it tuned back in. Intuition can be that way, too. One day you know every call before the umpire says, "strike!" The next, you can't find your car in the parking lot.

Sounds a lot like life to me. One day it's sunny and warm, the next the fog is so thick, your four-year-old daughter looks out the window and says, "Look! It's blurry outside." In short, there is a large portion of this *over which you have no control.* So you work on what you can, and realize that you won't be perfect.

I have been asked how it is that my guidance is so accurate during readings. I suppose practice and longevity has a lot to do with it. I've been reading for other people since that first automatic writing for Dad in December of 1988. That's a lot of readings, a lot of practice, a long time learning how to tune in, a lot of learning and listening and trust.

And I'll confide a little secret. It helps to have your back against the wall! While working my first psychic fair in Albuquerque in 1990, I was the "automatic writer." Others used tarot cards or crystal balls, or read palms. I used a pen and legal pad. People sat at my booth and I wrote down their messages for them. Once, after I handed a woman her writing, she asked if I could answer another question for her. She genuinely had something she wanted to know; I could sense she wasn't testing me and she would be okay if I said no. I thought to myself, if you're really a psychic, you ought to be able to do this. So she asked her question and I closed my eyes (it seemed like the thing to do!) and 'looked' for her answer. I shared with her the images that showed up in my mind's eye. And that was the start of my doing readings without the aid of a pen and paper.

The concept of having your back against the wall is why I assign partners in my classes and require readings to be done for one another. People will often be more willing to take a chance when someone else is relying on them. Human nature says we meet others' expectations of us, or at least try.

What Are the Psychic 'Radio Stations?'

People often talk about having a sixth sense, after the five physical senses. I'd say there's more like sixth, seventh, eighth, and so on. Pretty much, there is a psychic sense associated with each of the five senses, *plus a few more.*

1. Just Knowing
2. Gut Feeling
3. Sensing Danger
4. Hearing
5. Smell
6. Taste
7. Touch
8. Vision
9. Emotions

The vision and emotional senses will be discussed in later chapters.

Just Knowing

This sense is perhaps the most difficult to develop. While it can be pretty much "either you know something or you don't," there can be shades of gray between the two extremes. Usually, a thought just "pops into your head" and suddenly you have clarity. Sometimes you have this vague sense of something that won't quite come into focus. Practice will help you tune in more clearly.

I was having a conversation with an old friend soon after I had started reading professionally. He was fascinated with my newfound abilities and very open to hearing whatever messages might come to me. We were discussing his sister and he asked me about her boyfriend. In a flash I knew that the boyfriend was married, obviously to a woman other than my friend's sister. I hesitantly asked and he confirmed. As soon as an initial piece of information is confirmed for me, it is often followed by myriad details such as, in this case, what both relationships looked like (a codependent marriage, a karmic affair, a 'fatal attraction'), what the likely outcome appeared to be, etc.

Once you become open to these messages showing up unannounced, be ready for the floodgates to open. You may find yourself knowing that your next-door neighbor is going to move long before the For Sale sign goes up. Or your best friend is going to change careers when she is at the pinnacle of her current one. Or your daughter's teacher is pregnant. The list is endless. It can be as simple as knowing which aisle at the movie theater has an open parking space, or which company will be receptive to your resume.

It has been argued that so much of that is 'body language.' Maybe. I say, use every avenue of information that is available to you. Let the body language give you courage to say what you know to be true. "Your job / relationship / attitude is draining you. How can I support you?" you might ask a friend. You might just know that today was the last straw. Use that to help your friend.

Have you ever been talking to an 'upbeat' person whose smile seemed a little too bright? Or someone who said they were 'upset' but seemed to get a lot of secret joy in the retelling of their drama? I would suggest that you trust what you know to be true. Sometimes people lie to themselves. Not out of some sinister plot but because the truth is too much for their psyche to handle at the moment. In those cases, not only trust the information that you intuit about what is really going on with someone, but also take it a step farther. Ask Spirit what would be the best action for you to take or words for you to say to your friend. Use your intuition to know whether your friend needs a hand to hold or a little tough love.

Several years ago, there was some information that I felt I needed to share with some friends. It was pretty important to me, but I was unsure about sharing – whether or not I should disclose at all and if so was this the correct time? I prayed about it fervently. I asked that if I was supposed to share, that the opportunity would present itself and I would have a clear sense of doing the right thing. We found ourselves in the car together (an ideal opportunity, I thought). I started to talk, and my friend began saying something very negative about something unrelated. When we'd finished her topic, I tried again only to have her start to speak negatively about a different subject. I tried three times before I realized that

Spirit was guiding me, "now is not the time." So I backed off and let it go.

There is great power in trusting what you "know."

Gut Feeling

You have "trusted your gut" countless times. Oh, you may not have been aware of it at the time, but you have. 'Something' just doesn't feel right, you cannot explain just what or how. Maybe you actually feel it in your gut. Or something feels just right. *Intuition is a lot about trusting what you feel, even if you don't know how you have arrived at your conclusion.*

When I am teaching classes or speaking in public I always set my antenna so that I'm aligned with the highest good of all concerned. I find myself using examples I've never used before or bringing up a topic that was not on my agenda. This happens when I am doing guided meditations as well.

A few years ago I had a dream that my dad died. It was very real and my gut told me it was a premonition. My brother had a similar dream the same night, although our dad was in good health at the time. Since I received this information, I trusted it and acted on it. I went to see my dad in July even though I had just seen him in May. There was no rational reason to see him more often than I usually did. But there sure was this nagging feeling in my gut that I really wanted to deny but could not. Trusting my premonition resulted in my spending his last Independence Day with him, and we created wonderful memories that I will forever cherish.

Usually, the intuition signals something less serious. A lot of people I have observed have psychic ability but call it business acumen. A friend I know worked for a loan company and he always knew which applicants would pay back their loans and which would default. He called it "good loan judgment," but I believe it is psychic ability. The defaulters would look just as good on paper as those who would pay, but his intuition told him when it was a good idea to make the loan and when it was not. Probably you know people like this, who don't necessarily feel safe with the label 'psychic' so they give it another name.

Parents are known for trusting their own intuition when their children's welfare is at stake. "No," you can't go to the mall today," you might say, feeling like a mean parent but trusting that your bad feeling about the outing is telling you something. One of my children is known for 'dodging bullets,' as I call it. The one evening he decides to stay home is the one where all of his friends get in trouble but he doesn't because he is safe at home playing X-Box. His Guardian Angel works overtime!

Which brings us to the next area of intuition that shows up just when you need it...

Sensing Danger

My first memory of this was in college late one evening while visiting another university and leaving a friend's dorm. We had gone to some clubs earlier and locked our purses in the trunk of my car. As soon as I felt the cold night air hit my face, I had a bad feeling in the pit of my stomach. It kept getting stronger and stronger the closer we got to the parking lot where we had left the car. "Something's wrong," I clearly remember thinking and don't recall if I said it aloud. When we got to the car, my instincts proved correct. The trunk had been broken into and the purses were gone.

If I had received the information in advance, while it would have been very helpful, I'm not sure I was at a point in my life where I would have trusted it. So tune in and realize that when you *avoid* danger, you may never know what might have happened if you had... gone a different way home, ...left earlier or later, ...taken a job, ... spoken up or not spoken up,

Last night, for example, was not my night to be in an auto accident. I took the back roads rather than the highway on my way home from leading a meditation at a local church. Enjoying the warm summer night with few cars on the road, I cruised along. Suddenly a minivan veered across three lanes of traffic and then stopped sideways in my lane. I slammed on the brakes and came to a stop just inches from her van. In my heart I know that what happened defied the laws of physics. There simply was not enough room for me to stop without hitting her, but I did. Thinking about it afterward, I wondered why I felt guided to take that path home, then I realized, no harm done. There was no accident. . *Kept out of harm's way.* Your guardian angels have been keeping you out of harm's way your entire life whether or not you realize it.

Once I witnessed this in my brother's dog. We were picnicking in the park when she unexpectedly stood up and looked at the road, the hair actually standing up on her back. She started slowing backing up, putting herself between the road and us. Moments later a car came flying around the corner, lost control, and stopped a short distance from our picnic table. None of us can recall hearing anything unusual, although her keen canine hearing may have, but she certainly knew something was up.

So when you sense danger, it can feel like the hair raising on the back of your neck or a low-level jolt of electricity or just a pang in the pit of your stomach, trust it and act accordingly. *Listen to your instincts and err on the side of caution.*

Hearing

Now we're getting to the 'stations' that correlate with your five natural senses. "I heard a voice." Sometimes we hear it as though it is spoken out loud, other times we 'hear' in our "mind's ear" ... a word, an idea, a message. Be assured, there is definitely a difference between the voices inside the minds of those who have mental illness, and the voices of your intuition. Chances are unless those voices are instructing you to commit a crime or hurt someone, they are your Spirit guides. Common sense is the key, of course.

The Out-Loud Voice

Once my brother was hooking up a car to tow it out of a snow bank on the side of the road. He was between his truck and the car. Suddenly he heard a voice yell, "Run!" He bolted across the street moments before another car came around the bend and crashed into the stuck car. If my brother had stayed, he would have been crushed between his truck and the car, which was badly damaged. When he walked back across the street to the accident scene, he asked the owner of the first car, "Who yelled 'Run'?"

"What are you talking about?" came the reply. While the voice was very loud and urgent to my brother, no one else heard it. We suspect it was my mother who had been dead for a few years, looking out for her son. To this day he insists he heard the voice out loud, and I'm sure he did.

The Inside-Your-Head Voice

Sometimes the voice sounds like that same voice we converse with when we talk to ourselves. I think this is the psychic voice most people hear. The one that says, "Shhh" when you're about to say something you might regret later. *The one that tells you to trust yourself.*

Once when I was driving cross-country, that inner voice told me to switch drivers at 2 am. I didn't see a desirable place to pull over, though, so I kept barreling through the night at 80 miles per hour. At 2:05 am, I passed a state trooper who was more than happy to collect on my transgression. If I had listened to my inner direction, it is likely that either he would have found someone else to give the ticket to, or it would have gone to the other driver in our car instead of me!

I had a conversation once with the husband of the first psychic I ever saw in Cincinnati, a woman who helped me a great deal with just a few conversations. We would go to see her in groups of two to four, and while one person was getting a reading the rest of us would have enlightening talks with the psychic's husband. He was very intuitive himself and would entertain us with stories. He knew a person, he said, whose telephone rang and when they answered, on the other end of the line was someone who had died. The two had a brief meaningful conversation, he continued. We were incredulous as he assured us that it had indeed happened to someone he actually knew.

Some months later I had a similar experience except instead of the phone actually ringing, it happened in my 'psychic ear.' When my second child was just 14 months old, I suspected that I was pregnant with my third. While I knew that I wanted to have another baby, the timing wasn't great. A 14-month-old, especially one who was still getting up at night and having ear infections and allergies, is still a baby in my mind and I wanted to wait a while to enjoy this little blessing before the next one came along. However, the fact that I was awake at 5:30 am had me wondering, and I got up to get a drink of water (to quench another early pregnancy symptom). As I passed the telephone, I got this sense that there was a message coming to me. In my barely awake mind, I played along. "Hello?"

"Debra," a very calm, comforting voice said. My senses heightened. I became wide-awake.

"Yes?" I answered in my mind, thinking to myself, *this is the voice of God!*

"You're pregnant." I let out an audible breath, almost a sigh. "But I'm going to take care of you," the voice continued. I looked at the phone, still in its cradle, then put my head on the kitchen counter and cried with relief and joy. I knew I could trust this voice and all would be well.

When the baby was delivered almost nine months later, the doctor said, "Wow, that was a textbook pregnancy!" I had certainly been taken care of, as promised, and continue to be.

Smell

Psychic smell seems very real. When we smell something, it must be there, we think! Most often I have found this sense associated with loved ones who have passed away, although not always. What's fun is when several people smell something that is not there. When I lived in Albuquerque, we had moved into a brand-new house. No one had ever smoked there. One night not long after my mother, a smoker, died of emphysema, it smelled like cigarette smoke in my house. It was the first of many, many times when members of my family have smelled cigarettes in unlikely places (like church!) and known she was around. For my sister, when she smells cinnamon she knows our grandmother is around, just watching over us.

If you have a loved one who has died, think about what scent would remind you of that person. Chances are you have picked up on it when the source of the aroma was not visible, because the source was your loved one. Our loved ones do watch over us, and are invisibly around us.

Sometimes, the scent-message centers around someone who is alive. A client of mine in Albuquerque said she could smell her daughter's perfume whenever her daughter needed her. Invariably, the mother would call and the daughter would say, "How did you know I needed help?"

While I do not personally know anyone who works in the perfume industry, I am certain that when someone says,

"They just have a nose for it," there is more to their olfactory ability than meets the nose – a sense perhaps of the energy surrounding the scent, or its potential in the marketplace.

I think the possibility to receive insight exists even when someone asks, "Does this milk smell bad to you?" Your intuition is not reserved for only monumental events. *Pay attention. Messages are all around you.*

Taste

While psychic taste is not something I can remember experiencing, I can't rule it out. Just like the scent-testers, taste-testers most likely have an intuition regarding the bigger picture. "This product will appeal to the market we are trying to reach," they may say although there is no logical explanation as to why they know it. And even if there are some statistics involved, I guarantee there's inner knowing as well. I also suspect that there are those who can pick up on things that supposedly have no taste, such as poisons or chemicals, although I currently have no proof. (Maybe I have read too many Agatha Christie novels!)

And then again, we have the milk example from above taken one step further. If something does not taste right, don't eat it!

Touch

Over the centuries, fortunetellers have been known to use this sense, asking to touch an object that belongs to the client, or belonged to the deceased if they wanted information about someone who had passed away. It is certainly fun to practice with objects that people give to you. My friend Kevin is quite good at holding an object and "telling a story" about either its owner or its history. In my work, however, this is not something I use very often to gain information, simply because my other senses work so much better.

My daughter used her sense of touch once while shopping at the age of eight. She planned to use some of her birthday money from relatives to buy herself a doll. There was a hidden prize inside some of the dolls, a free gift certificate for another "twin" doll. As she searched, she picked up one, then another. She had settled on one and then impulsively put it down and asked me to reach one high on the shelf. She held it for a moment and then said, "This is the one." When we got home, not only did she get the gift certificate for the twin doll, but a bonus one for another doll, a triplet! Hence, "Michael, Michelle, and Melissa" were born – and she didn't even like dolls! I watched her closely while she was shopping and she was clearly relying on her sense of touch to "feel" which one had the hidden bonus inside the box.

My friend Robert says he uses a sense of touch or feeling to locate lost objects. While he doesn't actually touch something with his fingers, he instead feels a sensation in his body. He had lost his keys, which he knew were in his house somewhere. He stood in one room and asked Spirit to literally point him in the right direction. He could feel a pulling/pushing sensation in his body, which he followed down the stairs and right to where his keys had fallen out of his pocket!

Energy Work

While I devote a later chapter to energy work and healing, I want to mention that people, especially energy workers, can use their sense of touch to pick up on what is going on in other people's bodies. Energy work often involves the worker gently placing their hands on clients while they work on them. As they do so, they can actually feel dissonance in their hands, sometimes describing it like static electricity or a push-pull like you feel when you put two magnets together alternating positive-positive with positive-negative.

More often for me, I can feel it when a person really wants to accept the energy coming through me to them. Once I worked on a friend who had hepatitis C. When I placed my hands on his back, it was as though the energy was rushing through my hands and he was soaking it up like water in the desert. He remarked about it, too, "Wow! I can really feel it," he said. But the best part came a few weeks later when he got the results back from his latest liver tests and his numbers were better than they ever had been, having returned to normal levels.

When I use my psychic ability to 'diagnose,' I mentally tune in and scan the person's body in my mind. Then I feel in myself or see in my mind's eye what is going on with my client. I usually start my readings this way to allow Spirit to show us what is going on at the physical level. Since nothing is ever just physical, knowing that the person has excess energy in their chest might tell me they have a chest cold or asthma or sadness or grief in their heart. I use this often if asked how a person died. Sometimes I can feel the shortness of breath or pressure of a heart attack, which goes away as soon as I tell my client about it. Fortunately, my guides only allow me to experience others' pain very briefly.

This technique can also be used with a photograph of a person. Lightly pass your fingertip over a photograph of a person and if you feel a change in the energy, note where it is on the body. It takes some practice to be able to interpret the information you gain, so keep at it. When I tried this with a photo of my mother, my finger felt repelled when it was above her chest, as though demonstrating the energy of the emphysema, which took her life. As I was writing this, I decided to try it out on some family photos. When I scanned my brother, I felt some static at the level of his ears. I called and asked him and he had an earache! You can also try it with photos of people at different ages, to see what was going on in their bodies at those times.

In A Nutshell

Now that you have learned about the psychic radio stations, have you begun to see which ones come in stronger than others? Perhaps your Just Knowing station provides a louder signal than your Gut Feeling. Maybe you can Sense Danger better than you can tune in to a psychic Smell. Have you begun to Hear voices – either the ones in your head or the ones that actually seem like they are spoken aloud? Maybe you have experimented with psychometry, holding an object in your hand and allowing messages to come to you. Or perhaps you have tuned in to a person's energy field and allowed yourself to pick up on whatever might be going on in their body. The photograph technique, scanning a picture with your finger, can also be helpful.

Chapter Three Exercises

1. Start taking notes of when you receive information. No need to share it with anyone, but pay attention to how you get the messages:

- Just Knowing
- Gut Feeling
- Sensing Danger
- Hearing
- Smell
- Taste
- Touch
- Vision
- Emotion

Just Knowing Here are some things I feel that have just popped into my mind:

_____

_____

Gut Feeling I can't explain why, but I have a sense that...

_____

_____

Sensing Danger What did you feel?

_____

_____

Hearing – Outside voice "I could swear I just heard someone say..."

_____

_____

Inside-Your-Head voice "What I heard in my mind was..." Ask your Spirit Guides some questions and see if you can 'hear' their answers

_____

_____

Smell Think about a deceased loved one and see if any phantom scents show up. Or see if you smell anything that does not seem to have a physical source

_____

_____

Taste Do you have any examples of when your psychic taste buds kicked in?

_____

_____

Touch If you have someone who will help you, you can test this with questions, such as... "One of my knees is hurting. Lightly place your hand on each knee and see if you can tell which one it is."

_____

_____

2. Examine photographs of people you know to see if you pick up on any energy variations, then see if you can figure out what you were sensing

*I encourage you to
be persistent.*

4
Psychic Vision

P sychic vision is what most people think of when they think of "looking" into the future. Consider the commercials where the fortune-teller says, "I see a tall handsome stranger" in your destiny. *Keywords? I see.* When I bridged from doing just automatic writing to other forms of divination, psychic vision was the first sense I utilized.

Breaking it down into three different aspects of psychic vision makes it easier to explain and to understand. Of course all psychic vision stems from the same place – Source.

Three Types of Psychic Vision
  1. "Seeing" outside of you
  2. Third-eye vision
  3. Your mind's eye

1. "Seeing outside of you", or seeing what's not there

I'm not talking about hallucinations. This type of psychic vision is something that appears real but when you take a second glance, usually, it goes away. Often when people see ghosts, this is how they appear. If you are skeptical when you see the psychic image, the second glance when it's no longer as visible will confirm for you that it was just your imagination, and then you miss the message that was there. I've seen my share of spirits in my day, but they can still catch me off guard. I'll look up, from writing this book for example, and there will be someone standing nearby watching me! I'll look again and they'll be gone. "Oh," I think to myself, "just a spirit keeping watch over me and my progress." We'll talk more about our visitors from the other side in later chapters.

One of my favorite examples of seeing something that clearly was not there came during a psychic fair. A regular client came up to my table to say hello and just as plain as if it had actually been drawn there, was the word 'Wednesday' on her forehead. I laughed and told her, "You have the word Wednesday written across your forehead!" She didn't *really* have the word there, but the psychic presence was so strong, it sure looked like it.

She laughed, too, and said, "Well, I don't know what Wednesday is, but on Monday I'm going to sign a contract to start a new business." I wished her good luck and she went on her way. Wednesday afternoon she called me, very excited. "You're not going to believe this," she began. "On Monday, my lawyer had to postpone the signing until Tuesday, then again on Tuesday to Wednesday. If I had not seen you and received your message over the weekend, I would have cancelled the deal altogether feeling certain that the two delays were a sign that I should not proceed. Instead, I felt confident that it was right since you had seen Wednesday so clearly. So, thank you for that message!"

Other times I've seen expressions in photographs that seem to change while I'm discussing the people involved. I was reading for a woman who brought a photo of her family. At first we discussed her husband's relationship with her children, his stepchildren, and he looked very kind and loving. She confirmed that she was delighted that they all get along so well. Then the conversation turned to the couple's relationship. It was as though I were looking at a different photograph. When I looked at the man, he appeared stern and forbidding. I could see in his expression that he was very controlling with his wife and I told her as much. She admitted she was very unhappy in the relationship because he "kept her on such a short leash." *I was incredulous at how Spirit used the photograph to portray the information to me.* You may also find, either in looking at pictures or in real life, that things appear differently than you know that you actually are. I encourage you to pay attention to how things appear and make note of the differences.

What about things that are invisible, or things I have lost?

A discussion about seeing things that aren't there would not be complete without touching on the opposite or *not* seeing things that *are* there or should be there. Consider the word 'invisible.' It means not visible. You cannot see it. *It does not mean, "it does not exist," only that you can't see it.* Usually when you have misplaced something, it still exists somewhere, only you don't know exactly where that is.

On several occasions, I have seen things seem to disappear after someone dies, and I have no explanation for it. After my grandfather died, whenever we went to his house where my brother was still living, our keys would go AWOL and it took a long time to find them. Eventually they would appear in a place where we had searched more than once, often in plain sight! It became so comical that we began to say, "Everyone look. I'm putting my keys on the piano." And then when it came time to leave, they would no longer be there. Finally we learned to say, "Papa, stop hiding our keys and help us find them," and they would show up. It was as though once we acknowledged him, his ruse was up and he ended the game. Right now, my dad is playing the same game with my daughter's keys. I try not to laugh.

If you can't think of anyone who has recently died who would want to get your attention and whom you can ask for assistance, I have a couple other techniques I recommend for recovering lost items.

Finder's Technique for Yourself

Ask your Spirit guides to help you find it, then go about your day. I realize that sometimes you are on a deadline and need to leave *now* but try it sometime when you have a few moments to spare. Invariably, when I allow myself to get distracted and figure I'll throw in a load of laundry while I'm waiting, somewhere between that thought and the washing machine, I recover my lost item.

I have become rather philosophical about lost items. 'Hiding' things from us or creating obstacles is another way for Spirit to communicate with us. Just yesterday a friend of mine was telling me how the prescription she had ordered a month prior had been lost in the mail and she never received it. Then after she spent an hour on the phone with the pharmacy, it was again not sent to her as promised. It was after the third call and being left on hold for a very long time that she stopped to consider that perhaps Spirit was trying to tell her something.

Previously, she has been pondering if she still needed to be on the medication and had prayed and meditated about it, asking for a clear sense of direction. By this time, she had been almost 2 weeks without it and had gotten through the worst of the withdrawal symptoms. She talked it over with her doctor who agreed maybe it was time to stop the medication. She chuckled when telling me the story of how many ways Spirit had blocked her from continuing on the drug before she understood the message.

The more opportunities we provide ourselves to hear messages from Spirit, the more secure we will feel and the better connected we will be with the universal life force. When we ask for a message and then don't wait to hear the answer, it's like not getting the mail or checking our inbox. I suspect you are like me in wanting to help your friends, that you would eagerly check the mailbox if you were expecting something that would assist or support a loved one. Which brings us to my second method.

Finder's Technique to Help Others

Have your friend name the lost item (paperwork, keys, jewelry) and describe it. Close your eyes and try to get a picture of the item itself, then 'clear the screen' and allow whatever picture comes to mind next. It might not seem relevant, but explain with detail whatever you visualize.

For example, my friend had lost her airline tickets to Pittsburgh and called me in a panic to help her find them. This was back in the days of paper tickets, so without them she could not board the plane. I kept seeing an image of a beach at sunset. While I knew she wasn't going to the beach and it could not be where she had lost them, I told her what I saw (and tried to be as descriptive as possible). As soon as I spoke, she knew exactly where they were. She had been reading a magazine and had stashed the tickets inside while she was packing. The magazine was sitting on her dresser with a beach scene on the cover.

Once you designate a partner in this adventure, I recommend you practice finding things for one another. Be aware that Spirit will use your efforts as well as your words. For example, you might tell your friend, "I see the bracelet in your car, under the seat." Your friend looks in the car and the bracelet is not there. However, on her way back in the house, she finds it on the ground next to the door. Regardless of how your friend got there, the end result was that she found her bracelet, right? And you helped her.

Now that we have considered things in the physical world that either seem to be there even though our logical minds tell us they cannot be, or seem to be absent even though our logical minds tell us they should be, there is another type of vision that still focuses on images outside of your head.

2. Third-eye vision

"Third eye?" you may be thinking. "Last time I looked in the mirror, I had only two!" *The term 'third eye' refers to an energy center in the center of your head just above your two physical eyes.* It is one of the seven chakras, or energy centers, that you have in your body and are described in Eastern traditions. The chakras start at your tail bone with the root chakra associated with the color red, and go up your body along an imaginary axis through the rainbow of colors, ending with the purple chakra at the crown of your head. Studying the chakras is fascinating and I recommend it, but for our purposes here, let's consider just the sixth chakra, the third-eye chakra. While it is depicted in illustrations as being on your forehead, I feel that it is actually located more in the center of your head on that imaginary axis from your tailbone to your crown.

But where it is located is not as important as what it does. While all psychic vision is related to this energy center, I differentiate third-eye vision to be what people use when they see auras or energy around people. I have seen instructions on how to "open up your third eye," and have not had a lot of luck with those techniques myself, although if you find a method that works, stick with it. This area of psychic discerning is not my strong suit, although I have had moments when I have clearly seen energy emitting from a person and even heard a hum along with it.

My daughter, on the other hand, has been seeing auras her whole life. We discovered it when another psychic pointed it out to us when she was about 6. To my daughter, since it had always been there, it wasn't noteworthy. She called it "seeing colors." When we became aware of it however, we gently encouraged her not to feel odd and to use it to her advantage. She seemed a bit relieved to be able to discuss it and glad for the extra attention it brought to her. Once when she came home from school she told me, "I was scared on the playground today, Mom. Mrs. Anonymous's colors turned black."

I asked her what precipitated the color change and she said, "She was really mad at some kids." Still, despite her rage, all-black auras are extremely rare and usually indicate major trauma or mental illness. I was relieved that Mrs. Anonymous was not my daughter's teacher! Years later we learned that this particular teacher had serious mental problems that had gone undiagnosed. (We will further discuss how to encourage your children to develop their intuition in Chapter 7, Psychic Children, Animals, and Ghosts.)

So, if you weren't born with an innate ability like my daughter, how do you go about seeing a person's aura? There are two answers to this question.

(1) The best way I have found is not to "try." Putting forth too much effort only makes it more difficult. Relax with your eyes open and imagine what it might look like. Allow your imagination to provide an image for you and then see how real the image feels. Accept that an image might later pop in unannounced and then go about your day. I have also found that sometimes it's easier to see energy in the dark, when all of the messages going to your "two eyes" are blank, so your third eye can see without interference.

The method I use most often to "see" auras, though, is (2) to use my other psychic senses to pick up on what their energy field looks like. I listen for cues (I might hear "orange around the shoulder" for example). I feel the intensity and note what color it feels like, red being warmer, blue cooler. And mostly I use my mind's eye. I close my eyes and picture the person and allow the image of their aura to show up in my mental picture. It's an inner vision of their aura, and equally helpful to me.

Which brings us to the next aspect of psychic vision...

3. Your Mind's Eye

Imagine that you have a monitor (like a screen) inside your mind. Just like your computer monitor or TV, it has a variety of sources or channels and can conjure up all sorts of images. This is where you see your dreams at night, where you visualize things during the day, and where you can receive psychic information at any time.

Let's practice. When you're finished reading this paragraph, close your eyes and picture a rose. OK go.

Did you see the rose? If not, I encourage you to practice. You have inner vision; it's crucial to your survival as a human. This vision is the exhibition of your memory. Picture a route you often take, to work perhaps. The act of bringing this to your mind in a visual way demonstrates for you that you access your mind's eye on a regular basis, whether or not you are aware of it. Once you figure out how to bring images to mind, it will open up doors for you.

If you did see the rose, and in my experience the majority of people do, what did it look like? Was it a bud or a full blossom? What color was it? Did you see it on a bush? In a vase? Long stem? The exercise introduced you to your inner monitor, and this time you conjured up the image. When you look into your intuition, you will ask Spirit to create the image and then see what shows up. It's like tuning to a station and allowing your cable provider (Spirit) to supply the show.

Allowing yourself to see things in your mind's eye becomes easier with practice. Meanwhile,

M.S.U. — Make Stuff Up

Not really, but it seems like it sometimes! That's because you see it on the same screen where you see the figments of your imagination, and there is a similar process in bringing it to mind. The difference between your imagination and your intuition seems to be the source. One comes from you, the other comes from Spirit. I suggest that your imagination comes from Spirit as well, tendered through your intentions.

Once my dad was scheduled to have a past-life regression with a practitioner while he was visiting me from out of town. He had the session, paid his money, spent his two hours and came home empty handed. Nothing came to him during the visualization process, he said, and he was bitterly disappointed. The practitioner gave him a list of ten affirmations to recite to himself ten times each day. Then he was to come back and try again. While visiting us, he had planned a bus trip of the nearby region, so the timing was perfect for when he returned from his tour, before he left to go home. When he got back, the paper was creased and well worn and I could tell he had done his homework. On our way to his second session I told him, "Dad if nothing comes to you, *make it up!* You are going to pay for the session either way, so you may as well come up with something." It was the best idea I could come up with to encourage his giving himself permission to allow it to happen. My heart was in my throat when he got out of the car.

It all came together for him the second session and he was thrilled. He recalled a past life he had had with a high school girlfriend from this life that he had broken up with rather unexpectedly. He had often wondered why he had been moved to end the relationship, and his regression gave him answers he had been seeking for 30+ years. I saw a peace in him from that experience that warmed my heart, and I like to think my words may have given him the push he needed.

Meanwhile, I was having some of my own experiences using my psychic vision. I asked a young man to allow me to try reading for him without doing the automatic writing. It would be my first time doing a reading without a pen in hand. I chose him because even though I didn't know him very well I felt that he would not criticize me if it didn't work. I recommend you find a similar person. I took his hands in mine (because I had seen other psychics do it) and images started popping into my head. He was getting ready to leave for college in a few weeks, so I asked for information about his upcoming experiences.

"I see you in your photography class, only you're not paying attention to the teacher, you're looking at a girl with shoulder-length dark hair," I told him. Let me break it down and tell you just what I saw and how I interpreted it.

- I saw my own photography class from college. Since he was not going to the same university that I had attended, I figured this was Spirit's way of showing me his photography class.

- I looked around the room and saw him sitting in one of the desks, more confirmation that it was his class.
- Then as I looked at him, I followed his gaze away from the professor to the young lady.

When I mentioned the girl, he smiled and said, "Yeah, my girlfriend's going to take the class also and she looks just like that." While I knew he had a girlfriend, I didn't know what she looked like or whether she shared any classes with him.

I went on to describe several other events that I saw in my mind's eye and we were both amazed at the accuracy as well as the details I saw. It was my first experience with Spirit's language and discerning the interpretation of it.

Spirit's Language

There are endless images that Spirit can provide for you, and you probably see your share of them in any given day. *The key is to know how to interpret them.* Spirit gives us images that are meaningful to us. So if I see Miss McGetrick in your reading, I know Spirit is probably talking about your first grade teacher since Miss McGetrick was my first-grade teacher. Sometimes if I read for someone who shares some aspect of my own life, such as attending the same church, I pay attention to the images that involve our common ground. For example, if I see my client meeting a person in the basement of the church, I will tell them, "I see you meeting someone at church and I'm not clear if Spirit means the actual church we both attend, or if it means another church and they are using this image as an example." Description is very important in interpreting images. This is also true, incidentally, when deciphering dreams. When you express things aloud sometimes the meaning becomes obvious. Try it sometime.

Let's look at some specific examples of the *symbols* used in readings.

Places

When you see a place in your mind, notice if it is symbolic, such as a church or school, or if it is a location you can relate to, such as your grandparents' house. Also if you are trying to locate someone or something, try picturing a map and seeing if a spot 'lights up.' Or notice if you hear a name.

Once I was teaching a class and asked for some volunteers. I chose one of them as the subject and asked the others to see what kind of information they could intuit about her. I asked them to see where the woman had grown up. One of my volunteers said, "I know this isn't right, but I keep hearing the word England." Our subject gasped and said, "I am not from England. It is my maiden name!" While Spirit did not answer the question 'correctly,' the message was certainly pertinent. When you are starting out, observe and share all of the information you receive and sort through it later. You want to gather as much data as you can.

People

The same principle applies for people you recognize -- symbolic (your boss, neighbor) -- or personal (sister, parent). When you picture someone you don't recognize, it really helps to pay attention to the details. "He feels like he is shy and will hardly let me see him," for example, may be more helpful than "he is short and balding." If an image *reminds* you of something in your own life, pay attention. For example, "you asked about your boss and they are showing me a former boss I had who acted like this..."

It also helps to try to observe the setting where the person is in your vision. Clients often ask me whether they will meet the person of their dreams. When an image comes to me, I try to describe not only their appearance but also how the meeting takes place and where. *If you are seeing something, more than likely there is meaning to it, so pay attention.*

Situations

Often people will come to me with questions about how something will turn out. I ask Spirit to show me the most likely outcome, noting that people have free will and that circumstances can change. Usually, I will be shown several scenarios. "If you do nothing, this is how it looks like it will work out." And, "If you take this action, this will probably happen."

Once I read for someone who received very specific direction. First she asked me whom had possession of an item she felt belonged to her. Instead of showing me who had it, Spirit showed me an image of a room. When I described the room in detail, she immediately knew who had the item. What happened next was unusual. I clearly got the message to tell her that if she approaches the person directly she will never get the item back. The words 'always' and 'never' very rarely show up in readings, so I paid close attention to the direction I was receiving. I even asked Spirit to clarify and got the same answer, which I repeated to her several times.

I went on to say, "I can tell that you are going to approach the person to get your item back despite the warning to the contrary, which is regretful." She called me a few weeks later to relay that, yes, she had demanded the item be returned to her and now she is no longer on speaking terms with the other person involved. It drove home to me the fact that I have no control over what people choose to do with the information discerned in a reading.

Decisions

"Should I break up with him or give him another chance?" might be the question. I would then see what images came to mind. Chances are they would be events that I have witnessed that illustrate to me what is going on for my client. I might see images of a friend breaking up with her boyfriend or maybe another friend when she gave her husband another chance. Sometimes I ask to be shown the potential outcome for each choice. I relay as much as I can, always reassuring my clients that the decision is a personal one and they know better than anyone else what is best for their own lives.

I have been asked on more than one occasion to provide insight into a car purchase. A client in Albuquerque was convinced he would be driving a blue car off the lot, but that was not what I saw. "You will think you have settled on the car of your choice. In fact, you'll be walking out of the dealership when you see the red car and renegotiate everything." He scoffed at the possibility and hung up. He called me back the next day to confirm that it had happened exactly as I predicted.

Questions

"Will we have a baby?" I was asked this question at one of my first psychic fairs. I closed my eyes and an image came to mind of the client in a green velvet maternity dress. There was a Christmas tree in the background. I relayed to her what I saw and she was much relieved. Another time, I knew some friends had been hoping (trying) for a baby for a while. When I saw them, the word September came to mind, so I told them. This was in June and they had their baby in September of the next year.

"Should I move to a new home?" When asked this question I ask Spirit to show me my client in their ideal location and then describe to them what I see. If it's the home where they are living, I feel that is Spirit's way of saying, "stay put for now." If it's a new home, then we begin to get an idea of what it will look like and where it might be located.

Health

When asked health questions, I create an image of the person in my mind and see if Spirit provides any shadows or dark colors around any parts of their body. The darker the color, the more serious the illness, with black being almost a certainty that the illness will be terminal. I was having a long distance conversation with my sister once and a thought about a family member popped into my mind. As I studied the image, I could see Spirit was giving us a message about our relative.

"I see a dark area around her lungs," I said. "I want to say it's lung cancer, but I'm not sure." My sister asked if it was terminal and I took a second look. The area was black, I relayed, so more than likely she would die from it. Since this relative had not shared her diagnosis with us, we decided to honor her privacy and her right to share the news on her own time, and said nothing to the rest of the family. We took to heart the privilege we had been given in knowing about her illness, though, and I made sure to visit her the next time I was in town. It was about nine months later that she told the family about her illness and about nine months after that she died.

I also consider the lack of shadows or colors to be informative as well. If I see no interruptions in their body's energy field, it is Spirit giving me the 'all clear.'

Blank Screen

Sometimes we don't receive the answers. A client at a psychic fair once asked me who killed her son. When I closed my eyes, all I saw was black velvet, a blank screen. Then the voice of her son came to me very clearly, "She does not need to worry about that, it is not her concern. She needs to let me go." When I told her, she became very angry and walked away. I implicitly trust Spirit to give answers *and* to withhold them when appropriate. Only God can see the big picture and know what someone will do with information once they have it.

A dear friend of mine lost her husband shortly before their baby was born. Even though I was in close communication with her all through the pregnancy, I did not foresee her husband's death. As I look back on it, I realize that if we knew, we would have missed the celebration and joy of the pregnancy in anticipation of the tragedy about to strike. As it was, she was able to have happy expectations almost until the end.

You will find that Spirit will establish its own language that is unique to you. As with any language, the use and practice of it will manifest its familiarity. Be open to noticing little quirks you might develop when you are "predicting." For example, I noticed early on that when I specifically used the phrase, "I want to say that ___, but I'm not sure," the information was exceptionally accurate. That still holds true today, especially in personal conversations.

Trust & Describe

As you develop your own ability to "see" the future, the past, or anything else that is hidden from you, there are two things to keep in the forefront of your mind – trust and describe.

Trust

Spirit has your best interests at heart. The Universe is conspiring for your highest good. It does not matter **where** you believe that the information is coming from...
- Spirit
- God
- Your Guardian Angels
- Loved ones who have passed away
- Divinity
- Universal Life Force
- The One Presence, the One Power
- I Am

...so much as it matters **that** you trust it. Or at least give it a chance.

Describe

Pay attention to whatever information comes to you, *in whatever form*, and then describe it. Either keep a journal or notebook for your own eyes only, or share your impressions with someone else. "I'll keep a mental log," you are telling yourself. Please don't try to keep this all in your head. *There is power in the telling, and in the describing, as you will soon discover.*

In A Nutshell

As you can see, your intuitive vision may take different forms. Sometimes it feels like you are seeing something that is not there, an image that seems to appear then disappear. Then there is the third-eye vision that involves a different type of 'seeing,' viewing auras and energy fields that exist at a different level than our typical experience. The other type of vision is your 'mind's eye,' that video monitor in your head where you also envision your dreams and visualizations.

You have learned a few ways to find things that are lost, both for yourself and for others, either by allowing images to pop into your head or by putting the whole business out of your thoughts to allow Spirit to direct you to your lost item.

Now that you have opened up to ways of receiving messages visually, you are learning how to interpret them. Spirit's language is unique to each person, so an image could mean entirely different things to you than to your friend. We discovered how to ascertain information about people, places, situations, health and decisions, as well as understanding the meaning of a 'blank screen.'

75

Chapter Four Exercises

1. Be open to seeing things that are not of the physical world. If you're feeling brave, invite loved ones who have passed away to appear to you. Make a note of what you've seen.

Have you thought you saw something but when you looked back it wasn't there? Describe it:

_____

_____

Once I saw a "ghost"...

_____

_____

2. Practice using your third eye. Look at someone, or even an animal, and imagine you can see an energy field around them. Sometimes it helps to look past them or even to imagine you can look through them. Write down what you see.

_____

_____

3. Practice the Finder's Technique with a friend. Write down your experience.

_____

_____

4. Find a partner for these next exercises. Or if you are marooned on a desert island, think about a friend while doing these exercises. Time to turn on your

inner monitor and see what you find. Remember it might feel like you are MSU, and that's OK. You are learning Spirit's language.

Try picturing...

A Person (someone you probably don't know, who may or may not already be in your friend's life)

Be prepared that they might not recognize the image *yet*. Also, since you are just starting, you might picture someone other than your intended target. This is where description is key. (For example, while trying to visualize a family member, you describe a man who turns out to be your friend's boss and Spirit has a message for you about him.)

A Place Notice the details, maybe try to see a map.

Someone's health Get an image of their body and see if you picture any shadows or light areas.

The answer to a question Ask Spirit to reveal potential outcomes to different options.

Trust the images and then describe them.

5

Psychic Feelings & Emotions

Discovering that there is a vast amount of psychic information regarding emotions has been extremely helpful to me in many ways – both for developing my intuition and for living a better life. Knowing what people are feeling has been key to understanding what makes them tick and what their blockages might be to living a happy life. Spirit guides the way for us, both in what we discern and how to use the information once we have received it. It was an evolutionary process for me that actually started way back in childhood. Even though we feel emotions in our bodies all the time, the concept was new to me the first time I heard it. My body could tell me what emotion I was experiencing? That little bit of information changed my life.

Growing up I had become expert at denying my emotions and pretending either that I was not having any 'negative' feelings or that what I was feeling was something else entirely, certainly not something that might make someone else uncomfortable. I didn't realize that emotions are not only a natural response to life, but that they define our experiences. My lack of emotions (or denial of them) colored my life in more ways than I cared to admit.

So the transformation for me went something like this. Let's use anger for our example:

- Anger is not ok for anyone. I never get angry.

- It's understandable for other people to be angry but not me.
- Well, I might experience a little frustration once in a while, but rarely.
- Maybe I do get angry. In fact, yes I do.
- Sometimes I get downright furious.
- Not only do I experience anger, but so does everyone else.
- I can feel and express anger in healthy ways that won't overwhelm me.
- How I feel and express my anger defines my life and who I am.
- While I don't celebrate being angry, it does show me that I am alive.

So what does emotional processing have to do with being psychic?

That transformation made it safe for me to experience my intuition fully. It was essential that I understand my emotions and myself before I could understand someone else. It was also a process of self-forgiveness. Now I see that everyone has something that they are holding in their "guilty" pile, some infraction or misdeed that needs to be released in order for them to move on to a healthy and more fulfilling life. When you think of it, you feel a pang of fear in your stomach. "What if someone finds out? What if someone brings it up?" Once we come to peace with our inner demons they lose power over us.

It's as though we can say to the old demon, "Go ahead and parade yourself in front of the world. In fact, why don't you get yourself on the evening news—or a twitter feed! I'm not afraid of you anymore." Incredibly freeing. And the irony is that most of what we hold against ourselves is based on inaccurate perception rather than fact.

Once a client confessed to me that she was afraid she loved one of her children more than the other or that she didn't even love the one at all. Yet when she talked of both of them, her love was obvious. Somewhere along the line she had picked up a shred of guilt because of her frustration that her child was very demanding as a baby. The guilt, like a weed, implanted in her subconscious and grew. Once she was able to express it aloud she could feel the truth in her body. Her heart told her it was full of love for both children, although we can never love two people in exactly the same way. She forgave herself.

It was the emotions she felt in her body that provided the clues and the answers. When she began to talk about it, she felt the fear in her stomach of being judged by others as a bad mom, and fear that she was, indeed, inferior in her ability to give her child unconditional love. As we talked about it, though, she could feel the huge love she had for this child filling her heart. And she realized that her fear was unfounded.

Emotional Release

Emotions are like energy waves that rise and fall as they complete their cycles. Think of someone telling you a joke. At first you smile a little as the joke is being told, then finally laugh out loud at the punch line, eventually allowing your smile to slowly fade back to neutral. If you can picture it on a chart, it would start at zero, rise up the scale to 10, then back down to zero. The cycle is easy when it involves a positive emotion like joy or laughter. But when the emotion is one we don't want to experience, we sometimes stop it mid-cycle, say somewhere around level five or six. All the energy stored up in the feeling that would bring it up to 10 and then back down again, is stuck inside you, stopped mid-ascent or mid-cycle.

Of course there are times when experiencing emotions is impractical, such as at work or school, or in line at the store. So when we feel it coming on, we nip it in the bud before it reaches full expression, telling ourselves we'll deal with it later. When later finally comes, it can look like indigestion or a headache or even gas! The emotion seems to fester inside, plotting for its release, whether through a good cry or a bout of the flu.

Spirit taught me this concept a number of years ago while I processed some grief. I thought I was dealing with it successfully until an insignificant event brought forth a disproportionate deluge of sadness. My heart felt like it was breaking over a small slight, so I realized that I needed to release the pent-up sorrow. Since I was in a safe place to experience and process, I decided to go about my day and just validate whatever emotion came up. At the same time, I slipped a piece of black obsidian in my pocket. I like to say that black obsidian (a shiny volcanic rock) is "not for sissies! It will bring up your emotions." Since it was my goal to allow the feelings to see the light of day, I reasoned it couldn't hurt and just might help.

Two distinct patterns emerged in the release process. One was a dull ache that didn't get too terribly unbearable except that it stuck around for about an hour. I just noticed and felt it. The other pattern reminded me of a labor pain. It rose very sharply, hurt a lot when it got to 10, then just when I thought I couldn't stand it anymore, it began to ease. Afterward, I took the obsidian out of my pocket and it was burning hot! Through the course of the day, I experienced each of the patterns two to three times. By evening, I felt relieved and peaceful, and I had the best night's sleep in a long time.

As you go about discerning and defining your emotional release process, I encourage you to place the emphasis on observation. Observe what your body is doing and what it seems to be telling you. Learning which emotions typically show up in the different parts of our bodies can provide a useful tool for you.

Emotional Centers in Our Bodies

So how do you know which emotions reside where? The following outline has been a mainstay for me. Please use common sense when you feel anything in your body and rule out a physical cause. While it may be emotional in origin, pain indicates a call for action and sometimes a trip to the doctor or emergency room. I am in no way suggesting that you take any of this information as medical advice, only as a tool for understanding. This chart is a guideline only. Feel free to explore how it might pertain to you.

In Chapter 10, In Practice, I will show you how the emotional centers correlate with the chakras. For now, let's take a closer look at each emotional center.

Place in Body	Emotion	How it Feels
Head, neck and shoulder	Anger	Headache, tension in back of neck, tightness in shoulders, stiff neck, tight jaw, toothache
Chest, upper back	Sadness	'Heartache,' shortness of breath, can't take a full breath, tightness between shoulder blades
Stomach, gut, middle back	Fear	Butterflies, indigestion, 'knot' in your stomach, tightness in abdomen or at waistline
Pelvis, extremities	Shame	Cramps, lower back pain, gas pains, constipation, diarrhea

Perhaps this information is already ringing true for you, and you might even be feeling something in one of the areas and contemplating its source. For example, I have tightness in my shoulders right now that I know is from swimming last night and not because I'm feeling angry (although maybe I should be angry at myself for swimming too far!). Probably the first helpful test comes from asking yourself, "Is there a physical explanation for what I am feeling?"

Once you become familiar with how your own body experiences and indicates emotions, you may become aware that you can also feel other people's emotions in your body. You already do. And that's what this has to do with being psychic. Once you can use your intuition to sense others' emotions, it gives you another level of understanding, which you can use to enhance your relationship with them.

Let's take a look at each emotional center.

Anger

Picture someone in a blind rage: jaw tight, practically foaming at the mouth. I think of the opening to the old TV show, Gomer Pyle U.S.M.C., when Sergeant Carter was yelling at him while the troop is marching during the introduction. You can see the anger spewing forth from his head, neck and shoulders! "Move it! Move it! Move it!" Sergeant Carter is a great caricature of anger, as though energy spews from the top portion of his body where all his emotional energy is stored.

Your Own Anger

At this point you may still be wondering about your own anger – when do you get angry? In polite society we use nice words to describe anger such as overwhelmed, stressed, and disappointed. There are degrees of every emotion. For anger they range from frustration to disgust to fury, and cover every base in between. You can tell in your jaw at the end of a harrowing day just how much anger you have had to stuff in the course of your experiences. Maybe you wake up in the morning having to pry your jaws apart from clenching them so tightly all night long. Maybe you get headaches every time you have to visit your in-laws and deal with their annoying cat.

And in case you still cannot relate to stress as a form of anger, let me explain it more fully. When we are feeling stressed, overwhelmed, it is because there is too much going on. Even if we chose our blessings (to have 5 kids under the age of 6, for example), we can still feel stressed by immediate circumstances. Feeling stressed does not mean someone is a bad person or even made bad choices. It means that life is coming at us too quickly and we are angry about it. Compare the messages that come at you in the average day to what your grandmother experienced at your age. How could you not feel stressed -- i.e., angry -- that so much is being demanded of your attention? Of you?

Becoming aware of your own emotions can be amazingly freeing. Not only do you have a right to feel what you are feeling, you have an obligation to yourself, I believe, to validate your own emotions. Emotions are your natural response to life. How you feel about things defines your personality. What you do with your feelings defines your life.

Someone Else's Anger

Being aware when someone else is feeling angry can be very helpful, whether it is the clerk at the store (go to another register!) or your mother ("I hate it when Mommy brushes my hair when she's mad at Dad!"). You then have a choice about how you will respond to their anger, with a little advance warning. For example, take an ordinary day when you're feeling pretty much neutral. Your marriage is going well, kids are happy, etc. Your spouse comes home and you can feel your neck tightening up. You recognize anger but also know that you have no reason to feel angry. Most likely you are picking up on your spouse's anger about something. Maybe the ATM ate the debit card, or the car is acting up. Whatever it is, your advance knowledge of the other person's anger can prepare you to deal with it, and not take it personally.

Keep in mind, often people are unaware of their own emotions and might not take kindly to having them pointed out. It takes a while for some of us to become comfortable with our emotions and we feel exposed when they are put on display, even if there are only two people in the room. However, perhaps you are being given the awareness for your own edification. Maybe your spouse needs some down time. Being aware of someone's anger doesn't mean we have to say it aloud. Giving the anger some berth to work itself out is usually a good idea.

Psychically

In readings, Spirit sometimes points anger out to me as a way of showing me things my client needs to deal with, whether the anger is their own or someone else's. I try to keep in mind that we are powerless to change anyone else, or even their feelings, but we can bring understanding and empathy to them. People get such a wide range of information during readings, and Spirit knows just what they need.

Right after I wrote the above paragraph I met with a new client whose marriage had just ended. Before she even came in the room I picked up on her anger. As we discussed it, it came to light that working through her divorce presented her with a great opportunity. Finally she could validate and release not only her anger at her ex-husband, but also the years of anger that preceded it. As Spirit pointed out different events in her life, she came to understand why she was so comfortable with such an angry man. She left telling me of her plan to journal and work through some of her anger with a therapist, and I felt gratified that Spirit had given me the information she needed.

Sadness

It's no wonder that sadness is called heartache because that's exactly what it feels like – a soreness in the area of the heart, chest, or between the shoulder blades in our back. This emotional area is probably the one most people are familiar with. It's a popular gesture these days, when a person is feeling sadness, especially if they are empathizing with someone; they put their hand over their heart as if to say, "Yeah, I feel it here, too."

Your Own Sadness

Sometimes sadness or grief sneaks up on us, especially when we have had a major loss in our lives and some time has passed. We think we're getting on with our lives but this heaviness in our hearts just won't go away. Or we have an ache in our upper backs, or can't seem to take a deep breath. It is crucial to validate yourself, make it safe for you to feel whatever wants to come up.

What about those times when the grief seems to be stuck there and won't release? It was recommended to me to watch sad movies when I need to let go of some sorrow. At first this seemed counter-intuitive. Why make myself feel even worse by watching a sad movie? But I don't think that's how it works. When we cry, even tears that are triggered by watching *Terms of Endearment,* we cry our own tears, from our own vat of sorrow. An outside source may bring on the release but the tears we cry are our own.

There are other ways, too, to release built-up energy in our heart space. Sighing works well on a short-term basis. Sometimes just touching the sternum with your palm can help your heart to feel safe again.

Keep in mind that I am in no way suggesting that you avoid going to the doctor if you have chest pains. Pain always has a message for us; sometimes it's "Call 911!" A friend of mine was going through a custody battle for his children and complained of pain in his chest. Fortunately, a wise chiropractor sent him to the ER where it was discovered that he had blockages in two of the arteries in his heart. In his case, the pain was both emotional and physical, which can happen if the emotion is ignored for too long or if it comes on very quickly.

Someone Else's Sadness

When encountering someone who has had a major loss, we have all had the experience of feeling heaviness in our own heart space. I think people are reluctant to attend funerals because they can actually feel the sorrow and it's heavy and unpleasant. But in those times when it's not so obvious on the outside what is causing the sadness, you can tune in to someone else's energy. Just imagine that you are able to superimpose their energy field on top of your own for a moment and see what you feel. It might seem like a weight in your chest, or pressure, a dull ache or a sharp pang. I can usually tell by the feel of it how long the sadness has been present. It seems recent if it feels sharp or keen like a fresh wound, still energetically bleeding. If the energy feels especially dense or heavy, it's probably been around a while.

Sadness and grief, to me, are the easiest emotions to validate because they are the most socially acceptable. We expect people to grieve, much more so than we typically accept their anger or shame. So how to validate someone when they are feeling sorrow? Do not say, "I know how you feel." You don't. You can imagine how it might feel, though and say, "Yeah, it must be rough." Or, "it's a huge loss." Or simply, "Aw. I can tell you are hurting so much." No one expects magic words to be spoken that will take the pain away. We experience our own pain very personally, hoping that in the process of working through it there might be some silver lining to the cloud or even just an end to the pain on our own terms. While you may want to relieve the pain of another, you cannot. One of the most difficult challenges of the human experience is to stand helplessly while another person suffers. Your presence usually means far more than you might imagine, so I suggest that you validate by just being nearby.

Psychically

I think Spirit points out people's emotions, especially grief, during readings because it is a basic human need to be validated, paid attention to, noticed. I remember my mother saying once about a baby's crying, "Oh, he just wants attention," as if it were a bad thing. We all want attention! It's the human condition. Not to say that the ways people go about getting attention are always healthy, but underneath the unhealthy methods is the yearning to know that one's existence matters to someone else.

During a reading once, I picked up on some deep heart heaviness and asked my client how long it had been since her husband had died. "Five years," she answered. When I commented on what I was being shown she said, "Oh no! I thought most of my grief was behind me." Spirit guided me to reassure her that the presence of more sorrow didn't mean she had not been working through her grief. In fact, the opposite was true. It meant that she was now ready to deal with another layer of it, that she was making progress in navigating the pains of letting go.

There are many ways that Spirit illustrates grief. It can feel like the heaviness already described, or like a balloon taking up too much heart space, like pressure or even a vacuum -- the opposite of feeling light-hearted and joyful. It's a bonus that as you learn to tune in to other people's emotions, you will also gain insight into your own.

Fear

Just mention public speaking and most of the population will start to get butterflies! We know where fear resides. It's called a knot in the stomach. People have been known to vomit when fear overwhelms them. Even a little worry can put "my stomach in an uproar," as my sister described it.

Your Own Fear

While again I would not rule out a visit to your doctor when you begin to feel uneasiness in your gut, it might also help to check in with yourself. What is going on? Are you fearful about something that might happen? Are you concerned about someone else – what is happening with them or what they think about you? Are you dreading that test you've been studying for or an appearance in court? You'll know when you've discovered it because when you think about it, the pain or discomfort in your gut gets worse. Now that you've done your detective work, what do you do with the results?

We've already discussed that the way to release an emotion is to experience it. While you are probably thinking, "Why would I want to feel even more fear?" please bear with me a moment. This technique works. When you are feeling fearful, bring your consciousness to where you are feeling the discomfort and focus on it. Imagine bringing all of your thoughts into your midsection. How does it feel? Dull? Intense? Gripping? Notice if it seems to expand or if stays constant. Give it your undivided attention. Feelings are like children. They want your attention and they want it now. Give it to them and they move on to another activity. Try to put them off and they become more and more persistent. They won't leave you alone until you pay attention to them.

When we truly experience an emotion, it moves, comes to life. Sometimes it seems to get worse before it gets better. Remember the energy wave? The emotional energy starts at zero (neutral), rises to its peak and then lowers back to zero. If you stop it somewhere in the process, the energy to push it over the top is still inside of you. Its getting stronger is actually a sign that the emotion is releasing.

Trust yourself. You were born with the ability to process your emotions. Have you ever seen a baby who did not know how to cry? When you are in the heat of an emotion, you'll know it. Go with it. Fear can be tricky, however, because we are afraid of feeling afraid! I don't know of anyone who was actually scared to death, even though they felt they might die in the moment of sheer panic. We're not talking about terror or panic. We're talking about the quiet, stealthy fear that is very patient, waiting for you like a lion in the underbrush. Fear that eats away at the lining of your stomach. Once you face it, give it your attention, you usually find that the lion is actually a pussycat. It doesn't overpower you. In fact, it frees you.

Someone Else's Fear

While you may want to, don't try to talk people out of what they are feeling. Encourage them, instead, to feel it more intensely. Sounds like jumping from the frying pan into the fire, but you know better. The discomfort comes from holding on to the fear, not releasing it.

So when you are talking with your friend and notice that gnawing in your gut, as he talks about moving to a distant land, acknowledge that it might be scary for a while. Sometimes if we put ourselves in their place and say what we might feel if we were in that situation, it can create an opening for them to experience and work through their emotions. "Moving to Timbuktu would scare the beejeebers out of me," you might say. Then respond with the validation, "I don't know anyone moving that far away who wouldn't have some fear about it. It's a big change." Reassurance that the emotion is valid is a far cry from saying, "It won't be that bad."

Psychically

In readings when Spirit points out that a client is holding on to a lot of fear, the client and I are usually guided to follow the fear and uncover what else is going on. I remember a reading with a man whose wife had died. He talked about a woman who wanted to date him and his fear became palpable from across the room. As we talked about it, I could see his wife's spirit standing beside him with her hand on his shoulder. When I relayed what I saw he said, "Oh, I know she would want me to have someone else in my life. She even told me so before she died."

As he talked the energy shifted from his stomach to his chest. It became clear to me that his grief was too raw for him to consider a new relationship at that time. "My friends are encouraging me to just have dinner with her," he said.

"But you just aren't ready, are you?" I asked him. He broke down and cried tears not only of sorrow but also tears of shame.

"Everyone tells me it's time to move on, but I can't," he sobbed. We just sat while he cried.

"You'll know when the time is right for you," I encouraged. "We are the best experts on ourselves no matter how well-meaning our loved ones may be." I think he came for the reading simply because he needed to be acknowledged and his feelings honored. What a privilege it is for me to be in a position to offer that.

Shame

Now here's a tricky emotion. On the one hand hardly anyone wants to admit to feeling ashamed because it's, well, shameful. On the other hand, once acknowledged, it vanishes. As soon as we are ready to own up to feeling ashamed, we are also ready to release it. However, if someone else says, "Shame on you," the feeling can linger, especially if we privately agree with them or if our parents used shame as a discipline technique. If you heard "you should be ashamed of yourself" multiple times as a child, this section is for you.

Try not to confuse shame with guilt. Guilt is an indictment, a thought or judgment not an emotion. Sometimes people use the word guilt as a more socially acceptable way to describe their shame. Try saying both words to yourself. Guilt does not have the same charge that shame does. The truth of feelings is revealed in the energy attached to them.

Your Own Shame

We detest feeling ashamed, even more than we dislike the other emotions. Shame implies that we did something wrong, which is not always the case. I knew a man whose adult children were repeatedly getting in trouble with the law. Although he wasn't the one in jail, he was the one feeling ashamed, as though it were somehow his fault.

Lower back pain, cramps, leg aches, and bowel problems can reflect hidden shame. Not to say that every time a person has gas pains, they are harboring some unresolved disgrace. It's the other way around. If you want to see what emotion is dogging you and the discomfort shows up in your pelvis or extremities, chances are there's some shame in the mix. When you become aware it is, usually just the acknowledgement of it will give it wings -- that and a dose of self-forgiveness.

I contend that most of what we feel shameful about is an illusion or misperception. Just like the man whose children were committing crimes, we sometimes add layers of judgment to pain we already are experiencing. Once you learn how to sort through your emotions and let go of them, you might find yourself reluctant to add fuel to your own pain by fostering bad feelings about yourself.

Someone Else's Shame

People don't want to acknowledge shame, so you might not want to use that word in your attempt to validate what a friend appears to be going through. She's been to the doctor repeatedly for her chronic diarrhea but can't seem to get beyond it. You could gently ask her if she's feeling guilty about something. In this case, 'guilty' is a code word for ashamed. Words like humiliated, disgraced, and embarrassed can also unlock the door to the emotion behind them. Being clear that you don't see any evidence that she has done something for which she should be held accountable to a higher authority, you might make it safe for your friend to open up.

As I mentioned earlier, a lot of shame is rooted in misperception. So if you can create a safe place for your loved ones to share their perceptions, you may find yourself in a position to point out that really, it wasn't her fault that it rained today.

Psychically

When I pick up on shame during a reading, I try to be extra gentle. Once I read for a woman who had four children. Only I kept seeing another child in her aura and told her so. She looked at me in disbelief and I felt a stab of energy in my lower back, which I immediately understood as shame. "I had an abortion years ago, before I met my husband," tearfully whispered. "I've never even told him about it." As we talked, Spirit gave me a lot of information and insights to share with her. Meanwhile, she talked about her shame and then, just as I was feeling the energy move up into my gut, she mentioned her deep fear that he would leave her if he knew. By the end of the reading, she was a new woman. The combination of finally talking about it after so many years along with the acknowledgement of the feelings and the additional information provided by Spirit freed her.

Thoughts vs. Feelings, Drama vs. Emotion

Two things govern our inner lives: thoughts and feelings. We control our thoughts, whether or not we realize it. Our feelings are another matter. They spring up uninvited at the most inconvenient times. The path through and past emotions sometimes involves working with both your thoughts and feelings.

Pretty often, we believe our thoughts are emotions. A man just witnessed his son in a car accident caused by the other driver running a red light. When asked later how he was feeling, he replied, "That guy should have his license taken away. He has no business on the road!" An understandable response, but that's not how he *feels*. That's what he thinks. How he feels, obviously, is angry. Unfortunately, when we present thoughts as feelings, it only keeps the feelings stuck. People can go on and on discussing events and disguising their thoughts as feelings, and wonder why they don't feel any sense of release afterward. They did not release emotions; they entertained thoughts.

A dear friend of mine likes to say how she's worried about this and that, implying that her worry shows that she cares. Worry is just a nice word for fear. But talking about worry is an avoidance tactic, allowing her to stay in the drama and out of the uncomfortable feeling. When she focuses on the thought (worry), it grows and she becomes more and more deeply concerned. If she would allow herself to feel the fear, it would release. I'm not purporting that you should analyze other people's conversations to see what they are avoiding. I'm suggesting that you look at your own.

So how can you tell if you're in the thought or the feeling? If you're in the emotion, you can feel it in your body. Once you key in to the energy in your body, it will expand or contract, enliven or release. Sometimes it helps to describe it in terms of colors and sizes. "It's dark blue and the size of an orange. Now it's light blue and the size of a lemon," for example.

Just as the earlier chart helped to name where the hidden emotions reside, the following chart will help you to translate what feelings are hiding behind your drama talk.

Drama	Example	Hidden Emotion
Frustration	"Why did I volunteer for this?"	Anger
Stress	"It's too much!"	Anger
Blame	"He is ruining my life."	Anger
Misery	"It's never going to get any better."	Sadness
Melancholy	"Life has no joy for me."	Sadness
Loneliness	"I'm all alone."	Sadness
Worry	"This is headed for disaster."	Fear
Victim	"Why does this keep happening to me?"	Fear
Abandonment	"He'll leave me eventually."	Fear/ Sadness
Guilt	"It's all my fault."	Shame
Hopelessness	"No one will ever forgive me."	Shame

The Turning Point

Occasionally the emotions seem to keep getting bigger and bigger, until we feel like we are drowning in them. This is similar to an alcoholic 'hitting bottom.' What happens when someone hits a bottom whether emotional or physical? Picture that same energy curve used to describe the onset and release of a feeling, only this time instead it of looking like a pyramid it looks like a V.

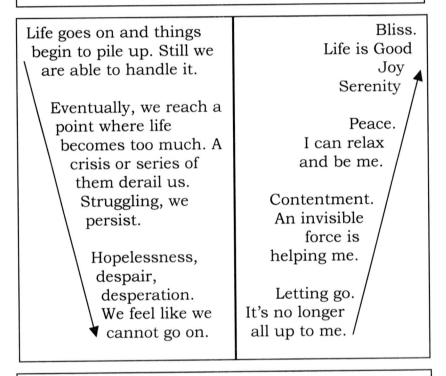

**We know our connection with Spirit.
Life is good.**

Life goes on and things begin to pile up. Still we are able to handle it.

Eventually, we reach a point where life becomes too much. A crisis or series of them derail us. Struggling, we persist.

Hopelessness, despair, desperation. We feel like we cannot go on.

Bliss.
Life is Good
Joy
Serenity

Peace.
I can relax and be me.

Contentment.
An invisible force is helping me.

Letting go.
It's no longer all up to me.

Turning Point—Powerlessness
We realize we can no longer do this alone.

Powerlessness is the turning point. In 12-step recovery programs they call it the first step. It's when we realize that not only can we no longer trudge this road alone, we were never intended to. We are ready to ask Spirit's help, give up the ruse that we are solely running our own lives. And that is when we make the turn for home.

On the way back up we find peace again, serenity, bliss. The more we call upon and rely on spiritual assistance the better our lives become.

Remember the example of my daughter and her reluctance to go to school in Chapter 1, *Overcoming Obstacles*? When we probed her emotions, we discovered underneath it all the primal fear of being alone. Our next step was to talk about faith, "letting go and letting God." When our backs are against the wall and we have no other option, we can find the best choice of all. To surrender. In war, people don't surrender to die; they surrender so their lives will be spared. It's the same way when you surrender emotionally / spiritually. "I give up! God, if this is going to happen, it's up to you. I gave my best effort with no result." Finally we are ready to avail ourselves of the help that has been there all along.

Often in readings, especially with new clients, I find this sense of urgency and impatience from the Spirit Guides. It's as though they finally have the audience they were seeking and all start talking at once. "We've been trying to help him, but he couldn't hear us." It is an act of courage to ask for help, whether from another person or from Spirit. Your mustering up the courage could open up possibilities for you that you could never have imagined when you were trying to be self-reliant. What is the first word of the Constitution of the United States? "We." When you realize that the human condition is largely a group effort, life gets better. You don't have to go it alone anymore.

In A Nutshell

As you have discovered in this chapter, emotions can be sticky business! But now you know some techniques that will help you to both release your own emotions and to support your loved ones in letting go of their own. Focusing on where the sensation is located can be a clue to just what emotion is lurking in the shadows. Remember – head, neck, shoulder = anger; chest, upper back = sadness; midsection = fear; and pelvis and extremities = shame.

Sorting through the maze of emotions and thoughts can help you to identify techniques you may be using to avoid experiencing your emotions. Whether it's blaming someone else, focusing on the worry, or replaying the drama over and over in your head, you may realize that you have become an expert at keeping the feelings locked away, all the while convincing yourself that you are processing them. This epiphany can be very freeing.

Which leads to the last concept of the chapter, the turning point. When you have tried everything else and are ready to give up, it is time to 'turn it over' -- surrender it all to God. Consider the simple phrase, "Let go, let God." Don't let its simplicity fool you. Therein lies a powerful spiritual concept. Ask for help and keep asking. Suddenly you will realize that your efforts are supported by visible and invisible means. I encourage you to prove it to yourself. What have you got to lose?

Chapter Five Exercises

1. Consider how you have felt emotions in the different parts of your body. Check in with yourself.

a. Are you feeling any discomfort in your **head, neck or shoulders**? What might you be angry about? Can you remember a time when you felt anger there?

_____

_____

b. What about your **heart space** in your chest and upper back? Any grief or sadness going on? Can you remember feeling it there before?

_____

_____

c. Check in with your **gut**. Feeling any fear? Describe it.

_____

_____

d. Is there any pain in your **extremities or pelvis**? Are you aware of any shame?

_____

_____

2. Look at the Drama / Hidden Emotion chart. Can you identify with any of the dramas? Do not be hard on yourself. Use this exercise to open up channels for your emotions to come through, not to criticize yourself.

_____

_____

_____

_____

3. Can you think of any issue or emotion that you can surrender? Imagine what might happen if you discovered that the Universe is conspiring for your highest good.

_____

_____

_____

_____

6
How It Happened for Me

A
t this point, it feels appropriate to fill you in on my psychic and spiritual evolution. Growing up, I wasn't encouraged to listen to my inner voice.

My dad became interested in metaphysical things when I was in elementary school and even visited a local psychic who had healing sessions every Saturday evening. Oddly, while each of my siblings attended with him at one time or another, I never did. My dad sensed that I had some gifts, and tested me with some ESP cards when my mother wasn't around to catch us. While I did very well on the tests, I viewed it as my secret gift that might come in handy some day, if I even developed it at all.

My first clear psychic moment came when I had my wisdom teeth removed at age 16, about six months after I had my tonsils removed. Back in those days, they required an overnight hospital stay before the surgery. On the night before surgery, I had a dream that the oral surgeon came to me after surgery wearing a yellow and green plaid sports coat. He told me that the surgery had gone well but my tonsils had grown back so they had to remove them as well. When I woke up they brought me to surgery where the doctor was wearing his scrubs and we had a brief conversation. The surgery went on as scheduled.

Later that afternoon, the doctor came to my room *wearing the yellow and green sports coat!* He was determining whether or not to keep me in the hospital another night because I was really sick from the anesthesia. I asked him if I had seen him that morning wearing the sports coat. He said, no -- when I saw him that morning he was wearing scrubs. "Are you sure?" I asked. "Then I had a dream last night where you were wearing that sports coat! You said my tonsils had grown back and you removed them, too."

He looked at me skeptically and said to the nurse, "I think we'll keep her another night." Many years later during a scope test with an ENT, we discovered that one of my tonsils had indeed grown back!

The 'Gift of Automatic Writing'

It was some years, college, marriage, the beginning of long-term sobriety, and three children later before I had my most dramatic turning point regarding my psychic abilities. A close friend had gone to see a psychic and allowed a group of us to listen to the recording of her reading. I was amazed at the accuracy and decided I needed to go see her myself. That was in 1985, and Sis, the psychic, accurately predicted several events in my life.

I went to see her about once a year through 1988. As I was getting ready to move across country, my friend Terri wanted to go see Sis but didn't want to go by herself. I had already seen her that year but reasoned that I may as well get another reading since I didn't know when I would be back in town again.

Almost immediately after I sat down Sis told me, "You have been given the gift of automatic writing." I had no idea what automatic writing was, but a gift had to be a good thing, right? She went on to explain her interpretation of automatic writing, which is that Spirit comes through the writer and expresses through the writing implement. She demonstrated for me with a legal pad and pencil. As she wrote, she never lifted the pencil from the paper, so there were these lines connecting the words. The message:

She is worthy of this gift. Instruct her well. ~Martha

Martha, she explained, was one of her spirit guides. She went on to describe how the handwriting could change during the process, and that she had even done drawings and other artwork.

I was awed and humbled and couldn't wait to get started. However, it was the holiday season and my days were filled with three small children and a husband who traveled. I was determined, though, and stole a couple of moments in the evenings. During my first efforts, I did exactly as instructed -- kept the pencil touching the page the entire time and just allowed my hand to be guided. It was a bunch of squiggly lines with the resemblance of a letter here and there. On the second or third night, I saw a word taking shape and realized that I knew in advance what the word was supposed to be. "Oh!" I thought, "Spirit is going to tell me what to write!" Once I became aware that the message would come into my thoughts first before it showed up on the paper, it became a whole lot easier. I have since learned that some automatic writers are aware of what they are writing and others are not.

The first message was what you might expect, *"Trust yourself and your guidance,"* something along those lines.

It was signed by one of my spirit guides whose name was so cliché, I was embarrassed and wondered if I could be making it up.

The second message was dictated to me one word at a time:

"Me and you are great together," signed by a different guide.

I was certain that I did not make up the second message because I would never use improper grammar, especially so blatantly! This same guide later misspelled a name that I most definitely knew how to spell, as if to prove to me that this was a voice other than my own. He also made me laugh, which helped me to relax.

When I sat down to try my hand at it again, my maternal grandmother came through. I didn't realize that I remembered what her handwriting looked like, since I was only 12 when she died, but as soon as I saw the letters forming on the page I knew it was Grandma talking to me. She was always very sweet, but with 59 grandchildren it was difficult to feel special to her. I was surprised that she came to me, and pleased. Her message, while certainly helpful was not so pleasing. We knew that my mother had emphysema, but she was still going about her daily round so no one thought she was close to death. My grandmother wanted to make sure that our family had time to prepare for losing our mother, though, so she told us that Mom was "getting ready to pass." This was in late December/ early January and Mom died in May. (I later shared the information with my dad and siblings, but my mother never knew about my newfound abilities. If she had, with her strict religious upbringing, she may have died sooner!)

Then my other grandmother came through, calling me a nickname I had long since forgotten. Again I recognized her handwriting and the loving energy that she emitted.

Over the next few days and weeks, I snuck in a few moments of doing automatic writing. My dad came to my house one memorable evening and wondered if he could ask questions and then I would get the answer through the writing. The first question Dad asked was, "Is there a devil to worry about?" Before I even started to pen the answer, I could hear the guides giggling.

"First of all," they said, "worrying about it isn't going to help!" They went on to explain how people bring the concept of evil or an evil being into their consciousness and, because they believe in it, it exists to them. But, no, they concluded, there is no negative force out there lying in wait for your moments of weakness. Dad seemed visibly relieved, and so was I quite frankly. It was something I had been wrestling with and I was glad to have it confirmed. He went on to ask about other dogma issues that had been bothering him, and seemed satisfied with the answers. He also asked if I could channel his uncle who had died, which I did.

My first attempt at gaining information for someone outside the family came later that same week. I had told my friend, Mary, what had been going on and I asked if she would like me to do an automatic writing for her. She agreed and came to visit. Keep in mind, this was all new to me and I didn't have a frame of reference for it. As I sat with the pen and paper in front of me, I asked her, "Who would you like to hear from?" By that time I had gotten messages from angels, guides, and loved ones on the other side, so I presumed that the same sources were available to her and told her so. (It wasn't until much later that I learned that most automatic writers channel mainly one entity and that it is fairly rare to be able to contact individual people who have died and then write in their handwriting.)

"I'd like to hear from my grandmother," Mary replied. I had never met her grandmother so I asked for her first and last names, sat for a moment until I felt that she was there, and started writing. As I finished each page and handed them to her, I could hear her amazed reactions. At one point she said, "I never told you about this, did I?" She hadn't. We were both impressed that I could access information that had no relevance to me personally.

What was most striking about this time, as I look back on it, was that pretty much one day I wasn't psychic and the next day I was, which made for some intriguing conversations with people who had known me all my life. After I told my youngest brother, who was brought up in the same traditional religion that I was, he said, "So does this mean you're going to go to hell or what?" We both laughed -- nervously.

When my mother died in May, I was living out of town. I knew she was in the hospital but the doctor thought she had a couple more months to live. It was Sunday when I did a writing from my guides who said, "Your mother is dying, go to her now." Now? Now, as in 'this moment?' Now as in 'today?' This week? Since I had already changed our flights from the summer to Wednesday, I decided that 'now' must mean as soon as I could get there. Apparently 'now' meant that day. She died the following evening.

When I got to my dad's house and got my children settled, I did a writing, which turned out to be from a dear family friend who lived next door to us when I was a baby. She told us that Mom "couldn't believe how many (people) were there to welcome her and she went happily and peacefully to them." She also told me that if I had been there, my mother would not have been able to let go and die peacefully. She would have held on to be with me. Her suffering would have been prolonged. I have since come to realize that it is a very strong soul who can depart when surrounded by loved ones. That's why you hear so many stories of people dying when the family leaves the room to go have dinner, or just steps out for a cup of coffee. My psychic abilities turned out to be very helpful to my family during that difficult time, and in the years following.

During that first year, one of the more memorable moments came when I did a writing for a friend of a friend. Her father had died a year earlier and she wanted to hear from him. I found a quiet place in the midst of a party and wrote several pages for her from him, a man I had never met. When I handed it to her she gasped then began to cry. "This is his handwriting! How did you know?" I believe it is Spirit's way of giving more validity.

As time passed and I received more and more requests for writings from acquaintances and people I didn't even know, my guides instructed me that it was time to start charging for my services. They even told me how much to charge. Thus I entered the ranks of "professional" psychic.

My First Psychic Fair

In the fall of that year, I met the psychic who would become my next mentor for the first few years of my professional career. When she learned that I did automatic writing, she insisted that I participate in the next psychic fair where she was also going to do readings. Within a few months I found myself sitting at a table with a sign next to me that read:

> ### *Debra*
> *Automatic writing
> *Channeled writing

I gave my writings separate names to differentiate between messages from spirit guides / guardian angels (automatic writing) and those from loved ones who have passed away (channeled writing).

It still amazes me how quickly my abilities seemed to materialize and then manifest in such a way that I was able to use them to help others. I learned so much in the process.

During my first psychic fair I did a writing for someone whose parents had been murdered. I was amazed and touched at the love and concern the father (who was the spokesman for the couple) had for his child who was so distraught by the manner in which her parents exited the earth. While I rarely remember what is said during readings, this one has stuck with me. He said that the murder was no longer an issue for them at all. Once they crossed over (died), they left behind all the negative energy surrounding the circumstances of their death. He went on to describe the vast peace that was their existence and asked his daughter to stop focusing on their last moments on earth and to know the truth – that they are blissful and peaceful right where they are.

I gained a wide frame of reference during those first psychic fairs. I became aware that while I was doing the writings, Spirit sometimes gave me specific words to write, as though I were taking dictation, and other times I would receive an idea and have to put it into words myself. I also discovered that Spirit has a sense of humor! One client came to ask me about her current state of unemployment. I became aware that Spirit was giving me dictation, word by word. "Your next job will be just a job, but the one after that will be right down your alley," I penned. When she read it she laughed out loud. She was a bowling coach!

Another time, the day before Mother's Day, a woman sat down surrounded by her children. "I want to hear from my son who just died," she requested. His message was very touching, asking his mother to allow herself to grieve and to know that he is in a better place. He told her several very loving things, which is typical. After I gave her the writing, she threw it down on my table and with venom in her eyes declared, "He didn't tell me the one thing I wanted to know!"

I couldn't imagine what else a grieving mother would want to hear from her son, so I asked what that was.

"Who murdered him!" she spat. While inwardly I gasped, outwardly I remained calm and told her I would ask Spirit. When I closed my eyes, I saw her son in a verbal exchange with someone else. It was very dark and when I went to look at the man who fired the gun, my screen went completely black. That had never happened before (and hasn't since) so I asked Spirit if there were any more information the mother needed. Again I heard the son ask her to let him go and allow herself to grieve. She was very angry with me when she left my table because she thought I didn't give her what she wanted. Sometimes what we want is not good for us.

I discussed it with the psychic at the next table after they left. When I told her what the mother wanted to know she said, "You didn't tell her, did you?" I explained that there was nothing to tell. My guides did not put me in the position to have to choose what this woman could or could not handle knowing. It was a huge lesson where my guides let me know they would protect me as well as my clients.

A Door Opens

As I read books about psychics and paranormal phenomena (sometimes they would even fall off the shelves at the library!), I began to wonder if I could do readings other than by automatic or channeled writing, if I could just receive the information in my mind somehow and then share it. This, I reasoned, would be far more efficient than trying to write it all down, and the clients would gain more information during their time with me.

Concurrently, a friend allowed me to try doing a reading for him without using automatic writing. I mentioned him in Chapter 4. The attempt was successful and I gathered quite a bit of information that was useful to him. Once it was proven to me that I could do readings without using a pen and paper, my technique changed.

Today I rarely do automatic writings except for my family and myself. I use the technique with them because it is easier for me to remove myself while I do the writings than if I am reading in my usual manner. Reading for loved ones is very difficult because we know what we want to see, and it is harder to discern if we are seeing that winning lottery ticket because it is going to happen or because we want it to happen. It is easier to allow information to flow in freely for my clients because I am not emotionally invested in their lives.

Early Career

It almost seems laughable to call those early days a career because I had few clients who came for appointments and only worked maybe three or four psychic fairs per year. I was blessed with a handful of clients who became very loyal to me. Meanwhile, I kept that part of my life from my neighbors and friends for the most part. It wasn't until I was moving out of that house and across the country that I came to tell my next-door neighbor about my budding career.

"So that's why that 'fella' in the Jeep has been coming to see you during the day!" she chuckled. I laughed too, wondering what my neighbors had been thinking.

We had another revealing moment in my daughter's third-grade class sharing time. Another girl in the class spoke up when it was her turn, "My mom went to the psychic fair yesterday and *her* mom (pointing to my daughter) was one of the psychics!"

The teacher asked me about it later. "That's so cool! Why didn't you tell me?" she wondered aloud.

While I told her I wasn't sure what she would think of it, the truth was that I did not want my children to have to deal with any possible scorn or criticism because of the unusual nature of my profession. I tried to shield them from those who would find reason to criticize because of their own judgments and fears about psychics.

Protecting my children was the biggest reason for my being secretive about it for many years. The turning point came when one of them came home from school on the first day of eighth grade and told of how they were supposed to share a fact about themselves that no one else in the class knew. "So I told them, 'My mom's a psychic!'" she declared proudly. I was privately relieved that the cat was out of the bag, and I think they were too.

Currently

Eventually I became more public and came to teach classes and lead meditations around town. While I still don't have a bumper sticker on my car that reads, "Psychic Onboard," I am willing to tell anyone what Spirit guides me to tell. Recently I was playing golf with someone I barely knew. He asked me about my job and as I got ready to tell him, it became his turn to hit and he headed for the tee box. After his drive, he didn't bring it up again so I let it go. If he had asked, I would have told him.

My openness to Spirit's guidance through my life, and especially about revealing this information to others, has protected not only my family and me, but others in my life as well. I had a job working for a public official some years ago. She knew what I did when she hired me, although she did not inform the rest of her staff about it.

My name was still on the Internet at the time for classes I was teaching through the local university, and I truly wanted to protect my boss who was already under scrutiny from the local press. A co-worker wanted me to put my name as the contact person on a press release. To explain my reluctance, I suggested she Google my name. When she saw the hits referring to me as a psychic she gasped and agreed.

To this day, I am amazed at how none of the local press picked up on the information, which could really have reflected badly on my boss who was also my friend. I repeatedly turned it over to God and continued to keep my name off of press releases that I wrote for a while, and eventually stopped doing even that. My name was listed (and still is!) on websites relating to my former job, and my name is found throughout websites regarding my psychic work, but no one has ever connected the two. I would not bring it up now except that it illustrates how God can and does intervene for us. My former boss has since died and I can feel her approving and laughing about it with me from the other side.

In a Nutshell

While I had been having intuitive experiences my entire life, just as you have, I can note a significant turning point when I was told that I was "given the gift of automatic writing," by a psychic that I visited. What that message did for me was give me permission to explore and experience the natural ability that everyone has, but in a specific format that felt safe and possible for me. Things moved very quickly for me after that, up to when I was a reader at my first psychic fair just about a year later. When I look back on those times, what is most notable is my naiveté. It simply did not occur to me that the automatic writing would not work for me, nor did I think to limit it. I was teachable in my innocence (or ignorance!).

Making the leap from automatic writing to reading without a pen in hand took a little more persistence and belief in myself. I read every book my guides put in front of me, and tried most of the suggestions therein. Having a track record, however brief, in tuning in while writing allowed me to consider the possibility of doing more. My consistent motivation during all of this time was that I wanted to help people, and I still do. It seems foolish to deny a talent that has the potential to bring solace to the grieving, encouragement to the down trodden, and guidance for those who seek it. At the same time, I expose myself to possible scorn and ridicule, or even worse. I am fortunate to have the support of my family and closest friends, as well as the multitude of clients I have seen since 1989.

The underlying current throughout my career, and my life, is turning to God and having faith that I will be guided and protected in every moment. Whatever your belief system entails, I am convinced that you need a sense of Something Beyond to open up your intuition. It matters less what form your belief takes than that you have any belief at all. I really don't think God cares what you call him/her/it or what your spiritual practice is, as long as you have a love for your fellow beings. Pretty simplistic, I know. We'll all find out someday.

Chapter Six Exercises

1. Think back to your first psychic experience. You have already had many. Jot down what you remember about it.

_____

_____

2. Try your hand at automatic writing. For you it may happen that you feel your hand being guided but do not know what is being written, or you may know what you are writing as you put it on paper. Rest your pen on the page and relax. See what happens.

_____

_____

_____

3. Now try automatic writing by asking Spirit a question such as, "Where do I need to concentrate my attention in my life right now?"

_____

_____

_____

4. Ask your guides to reveal themselves to you and tell you their names. What are they? Trust the first answers that come to you even if they seem silly.

_____

_____

5. Without looking at the caller ID, see if you can intuit who is calling you the next time the telephone rings. When you go to the mailbox, try to "see" what is in there before you open the door. Jot down your experiences.

_____

_____

_____

_____

6. Make a practice of asking your guides to give you a Word for the Day when you wake up. Try to think of your word throughout the day to ascertain its significance. Write down your words for today and tomorrow.

_____

_____

_____

7

Psychic Children, Animals & Ghosts

N ow that I have given you my own background, I would like to spend the next few chapters answering questions I am most often asked in the course of my work.

While it may seem odd to lump together children, animals and ghosts, I have found that they have a lot in common and that children and animals are often the ones who most easily see ghosts. And ghosts can appear as children and animals.

Psychic Children

People ask me if their children are psychic and I always have the same answer, "Everyone is psychic." Some people are born with more abilities to use their natural gifts than others, but we all have intuition. I hesitate to single out a child as psychically gifted because I have seen a number of parents use the label as a way to excuse themselves for not parenting their children. A 'gifted' child needs limits and consequences just as much as one whose gifts are not so obvious.

My first experience with psychic children happened with my own child before I had ever seen a psychic and before I had much exposure to paranormal phenomena. I was feeding my first-born who was about eight months old. It was the middle of the night and we were in the living room with the lights out so we would not wake up my husband. We stretched out on the couch with my back to the wall and her facing me. When she became still I guessed that she had gone to sleep and looked down to check. Instead she was wide-eyed and looking up at a blank space on the wall above the couch. Her eyes lit up and she widened her gaze and smiled. Then she raised her hand and whispered, "Hi!" I got goose bumps all over and a chill down my spine. I blinked a few times to make sure I was really awake. She kept gazing at the wall, moving her eyes as though following the movements of something/someone, and finally said, "Buh-bye." At the time she was just learning to talk, barely saying Hi and Bye to us, much less to someone I couldn't even see!

I asked a co-worker to tell her psychic friend what had happened and get her impressions. She said my daughter most likely had seen one of her own spirit guides since by that time in her life she had not known anyone who had died. The explanation sounded plausible but quite frankly, the experience scared me. Who was this being who showed up in my house in the middle of the night *and communicated with my baby*! It left me feeling shaken and a little unsafe. Thus started my quest of working through my fears and emotions; something that I felt was necessary to prepare myself for the possibility of future 'meetings.' And, I did not want to deny my children their own psychic experiences, especially since my first-born seemed quite pleased with whatever it was that she saw.

A few years later when I saw my first psychic, she told me that I had intuitive talents that had been discouraged as I was growing up, so I wanted to not only develop my own, but empower my children to have full access to theirs as well. I headed to the library and sought out books on the subject, which was my usual source for information in the early years. What I found was a wonderful book called, *"Is Your Child Psychic? A Guide to Developing Your Child's Innate Abilities"* by Alex Tanous, a book that is now available online. I highly recommend it. What I took from it was the message to treat a child's psychic experiences as normal, and not to go to either extreme of overemphasizing or scorning them. Act like it is just part of everyday life.

I had the opportunity to practice that when I was pregnant with my third child and my first-born was age four. I was getting ready to have lunch with my friend, Kathleen, and standing in the bathroom brushing my teeth. My eldest came in, put the lid down on the toilet, and climbed up on it so she was eye-level with me. "Mommy," she said very earnestly, "Kathleen has a baby in her belly just like you do." Now, while I felt like swallowing my toothbrush, I remained calm and said, "Oh, she does? How do you know?" My daughter just shrugged and climbed down, having delivered her message.

When I got to Kathleen's house, she answered the door with, "Guess what?!?"

I feigned ignorance.

"I'm pregnant!" she happily announced. "I just did the test this morning!" After we shared a few joyous moments savoring her news, I did tell her that my daughter had already told me. We both just laughed and shook our heads. Kids!

Children Seeing Ghosts

Children have vivid imaginations and sometimes they make up stories. Some adults make up stories, too. So how can you tell if your child is seeing an apparition or doing some creative visualization? As a parent, mostly you just know. You can feel it. And if you're not sure, ask *casual* questions such as "What did it look like?" "How did you feel when you saw it?" "Was there a message for you or for someone else?" You don't want to drill your child with questions to put them on alert, just show some gentle curiosity. Ask your child what their impression was of what happened. If it's a tall tale, it might grow upon the telling.

If your child seems very upset about it, don't ignore it. One of my daughters used to have night terrors and would wake up screaming. Whether or not she was dreaming didn't matter. She was terrified and it was real to her. I validated her feelings. "Aw, you seem really, really scared," I told her and hugged her tight.

She sobbed, "Ye-es."

"Tell me about it," I encouraged. And then I listened. It didn't matter what I thought was happening, what mattered was that I believed her. She talked about it and I told her that God and her guardian angels are always with her, protecting her, and that she can call upon them. We made up some prayers that she could say.

Eventually the night terrors lessened and gradually stopped all together, but before they did, she and I came up with all sorts of 'treatments.' We added a night-light to her room. I made a ghost-busting elixir using distilled water, black tourmaline and hematite. (Use a clean glass jar and fill with distilled water. Add some pieces of whatever minerals you want, in this case tourmaline and hematite, and let sit in the sun for a week.) We put the elixir in a spray bottle and she misted the areas in front of the door and window of her room before going to sleep each night. While this may seem like hocus-pocus, it was harmless, helped her feel a little less powerless in the situation, and just might have helped.

"The Lady is Scaring Me!"

My youngest daughter was visited by a spirit in the middle of the night when she was less than two years old. Unfortunately this one wasn't as friendly as the one who appeared to her sister. She woke up screaming and I brought her into the family room so as not to wake the rest of the family. I turned on a lamp, and she kept pointing into the dark part of the house saying, "The l-lady is sc-scaring me." Despite my efforts to calm her down, she kept getting more and more upset. Finally I admitted to myself that she must have been seeing a spirit who was trapped between earth and the hereafter. While I didn't see the spirit myself, I could feel a presence when I allowed myself to tune in.

By this time, I had some experience in these matters and knew what to do. I communicated with 'the lady' and through my thoughts encouraged her to "go to the light." As I did this, I became aware of a beam of white light coming down, inviting her to follow it. It took some convincing, but she eventually floated into the light. It then took my daughter and me quite a while to settle down enough to fall back to sleep. When I asked my mentor about it later she said that it was a vicious cycle where the lady, a recently deceased mother of young children, inadvertently startled my daughter with her presence and then wanted to comfort her and help her stop crying. When the lady tried to get closer, her presence had the opposite effect and my daughter cried harder and louder.

My Mother Visits Choir Class

Not all experiences with ghosts are scary. My eldest daughter has psychic vision that is extraordinary. In fact, if I can feel something but not see it, I'll ask my daughter to fill me in on what she is seeing. One afternoon she was sitting in junior high choir class. They had one of those pianos that were programmable so the teacher could record a passage and then replay it while she directed the choir. However, at this time the teacher had not recorded anything and was standing talking to the class.

A single note played on the piano, and then another. My daughter looked up to see (the ghost of) my mother standing at the piano with an impish grin on her face. This caused quite a stir with the students, who welcomed the interruption. We have never figured out why my mother visited the choir that day, but she continued to play random notes on the piano for a while. Then she went to the door, which has an automatic closer on it, and opened it. When it began to close, she pushed it back open again. While the teacher and the class were shocked, my daughter had to suppress her grin. Oh, "Betty Grandma!"

Penny, the Psychic Dog

My first Yorkshire Terrier had quite the sixth sense, which I've seen and heard about in lots of animals, not just dogs. Penny would accompany me while I read for clients. Once I was reading for a woman who was quite distraught over an impending divorce. Penny jumped up on the woman's lap during the reading and I watched my client calm down as my little dog worked her magic. Unconsciously, as she was petting Penny, it was calming her down. My sweet dog seemed to understand that her presence was needed, because she usually sat at my feet.

Occasionally, Penny would bark at things that "weren't there" and we knew an angel or spirit was near. One evening while we were eating dinner, Penny began to jump up and down and bark at the air, very odd behavior, as she was normally very calm. One of my children said, "There must be a spirit! Mom who is it?" Two messages came to me at once and I realized there were two angels visiting us: Michael, the guardian, was accompanying a little boy. When I closed my eyes the boy wrote his name for me to read, one letter at a time very slowly as they do in first or second grade. I said the name aloud as I read it and then we all gasped. It was a family friend who had died as a young boy. He just wanted to let us know he was okay, and came to us because we could see him.

Penny eventually calmed down for a while, but then started barking again when we went into the front room where the little boy angel had fun flying around in the two-story entrance way. The dog ran up and down the stairs after him, and you could almost hear laughter.

A few years later, Penny developed cancer and it sadly became time for her to leave us. I asked her to let me know when she was ready, which she did. She was so stoic, but I could tell she was in a great deal of pain. She spent her last afternoon comforting us and licking our tears before we finally brought her to the vet hospital. For days afterward, we could hear her spirit walking around the house as if to let us know she was running happily in heaven now, not to worry.

Psychic Pets

Occasionally I have clients ask me about their pets who have passed away. It amazes me how the animals relay their messages of comfort and give me images to share, such as showing me a favorite toy or food. While I was reading once for a woman who was bereft over her dog's passing, the dog appeared in my window. Her dog's image was so strong it made my own (real) dogs bark outside.

When you have lost a pet, its spirit is like a person's in that it will come to be with you upon request. Another client could feel the spirit of her cat jump up on the bed at night after it died. She said she even felt an impression in the blanket after it left.

The doorbell interrupted my writing just now. When I opened the door, there sat my two dogs, a beagle and Yorkie, looking like they had actually rung the bell themselves! My neighbor had found them roaming the street and was returning them. (Thanks, Charlie!) Apparently the gate had blown open and they "escaped" to adventures beyond. Interestingly, I was just about to write, "I have not seen too many examples of intuition in the beagle and Yorkie we have right now!" Maybe they were trying to get my attention and prove otherwise. Perhaps I've underestimated them.

You'll know *your* pet might be psychic if it...

- Suddenly pays attention to an area of the room where nothing is happening

I've heard dozens of stories of cats standing at attention at a certain time, only to find out later that something was happening at another location that affected their owners. For example, one of my clients told me that their cat "went crazy" at the exact time their son was in an auto accident in another state.

- Barks or meows at "nothing"

Just like Penny barking at our visiting angels, your pet can clue you in when a spirit comes to visit.

- Goes to the door *before* anyone arrives

Penny would bark at the door about 15 minutes before clients would arrive. At first I would panic that they were early and I wasn't quite ready, until I learned her pattern. I suppose that peoples' spirit guides arrive before they do and that Penny 'saw' them.

- Shows their dislike for someone that you later find out is less than honorable

I tell my children, "If the dogs don't like them, pay close attention. They are trying to tell you something. Animals don't lie."

So How Do You Interpret Your Pet's Messages?

It takes practice, just like I had to figure out the timing of Penny's barking before clients arrived. Take mental (or written) notes of what happens before, during, and after your pet seems to want to give you a message. With some persistence, you will figure it out. Or call a psychic. I know a good one. In all seriousness, about half of my clients come to see me because they think they need information about one subject, when in fact their guides wanted to provide insight in an entirely different area. Don't underestimate the ingenuity of your intuition. It will use whatever methods will work to get you where you need to be, even if it means alerting your pets to get your attention.

My Favorite Ghost Stories

An obvious question when a ghost appears is "Why?" Mostly, I can figure out the answer but there have been a few visitors to our house who have defied explanation.

The Little Girl in the White Nightgown

About eight months after I moved to Albuquerque my brother came to visit me. We were watching TV one evening when he said, "You know you have a ghost?" I sighed. This paranormal stuff was still fairly new to me at that time. There were many nights when I was the only adult in the house and I really didn't want to admit that I had a supernatural visitor. I had my hands full with the three children I had!

"Yeah," I groaned. "I thought so." At that point she would show up just long enough for someone to notice her, and then disappear. A few years later, though, she really made her presence known to my dad and me. We had gone on a day trip and everyone was pretty tired. My daughters were asleep and I had just checked on them when this little girl appeared at the opening of the hallway going back to the bedrooms. As soon as she had our attention, she turned and 'ran' back the hall, like a child would if she were not supposed to be out of bed. Her white nightgown billowed out behind her when she turned. Dad exclaimed, "Huh! Who was that?"

"Well, it wasn't one of mine!" I answered, getting up to check on my daughters to make sure. When I looked, they were all still in their beds fast asleep. Dad and I discussed it for a while but she did not reappear that evening. What was interesting to me was that when we moved from Albuquerque a month later, she moved with us. Most everyone in the extended family experienced seeing her at one point or another and we never did find out what her purpose was in visiting us. Then she stopped appearing, again with no explanation. We haven't seen her in years.

The Man in the Homburg

I was reading for a couple in Albuquerque when a man (ghost) appeared wearing a dark overcoat and a Homburg hat. I described him to them, expecting that he had some connection to one of them, but that wasn't the case. I apologized for taking up their reading time with this uninvited guest, but they were as fascinated as I was and asked me to continue to communicate with him. On a psychic level (which means the conversation took place seemingly in my thoughts) I asked him what he wanted. He was reluctant to communicate with me but didn't want to leave, either. When I suggested that he go to the light, he clearly did not like that idea!

I could tell that he was deeply ashamed of something, and from his attire I pieced together an understanding that he had lived during the time of the Nazi regime in Germany. When I asked my guides what he had done, they let me know that his shame was more for what he had *not done.* After some additional insight from my guides, it became clearer to me that this man felt he did not deserve to go to the light (heaven). I do not pass judgment on spirits who appear to me, leaving that to God, and instead act as a loving force of peace and forgiveness.

What happened next still amazes me. Since I was getting nowhere with my attempts to help him release, I asked one of my guides, an angel actually, to help him. When she appeared he transformed before my eyes from this large formidable, almost hostile man to a small broken, old man in a wheelchair. I 'spoke' words of forgiveness to him and told him it was okay, that she would take him where he needed to go. The look of appreciation on his face brought tears to my eyes, and he looked back in gratitude to me while she "wheeled" him up the ramp of white light.

The energy in the room was vibrating with an intensity that I can only describe as freedom and peace, and all three of us were speechless for a few moments. It was as though we had witnessed a sacred transformation and it touched us deeply. I still marvel at the memory.

The Couple in Arkansas

Several years after the Man in the Homburg incident, I had a similar poignant experience. I was in a dimly lit barn choosing quartz crystals to buy when I saw a man in overalls standing in the sunlight at the entrance to the barn. He motioned for me to come to him, which I did. He was so real, I wasn't completely sure he was a ghost until I got to the doorway and saw through him.

Once I got there, though, he just stood there looking at his feet, embarrassed and reluctant. I presumed he needed my help and asked him, again on the psychic level, what he wanted. His sense of shame was overwhelming and I could tell that he was tormented with a need to go to the light, and a belief that he did not deserve to go. As he stood there kicking at the dirt with his boot, I asked my guides for more information. I saw the image of a woman's body being pulled from a lake, and knew that he somehow had something to do with her death, although I knew he had not killed her. Again, it was something he *had not done* that troubled him, although I could not get a clear picture of what that was. It seemed like he had known that she was in danger and did not protect her, for which he felt deeply regretful. The guides told me that no one except himself had ever held him accountable for her death, and the forgiveness had to come from within him.

I tried for a while to convince him to let go with no result. I called upon the white light to come down and show him the way, which it did although he refused to go. Help came this time in the form of his wife, also a ghost. Between the two of us, we were able to convince him that it would be okay for him to go to the light. She took his hand and the two of them set off. They looked back at me many times and mouthed the words, "Thank you" and "God bless you." Tears rolled down my face as I watched them leave. It is unusual for me to cry, but this sacred moment filled me with such humility I could not hold back my emotion. I stood there for a long time before going back into the barn.

The Lights in the Family Room

My dad came to visit me shortly after "Aunt Frannie" died. My house was new and it was his first time there. While he fixed his customary late-night bowl of oatmeal, I showed him where the light switches were so he could turn them off when he was ready; I was going to bed. As was his habit, just as I was about out of earshot he would start another conversation, calling me back into the room. Finally after several repeats of this pattern, I told him to save his next thought for tomorrow; I was really going to bed this time. When I reached the top of the stairs he laughed and said, "Very funny!"

I groaned and went back downstairs to see what he was laughing about and he looked surprised to see me coming from upstairs. The light in the adjoining family room, he said, turned out and he thought I was playing a joke on him. "Must be Aunt Frannie," I said. "There is only one switch for that light and you could see it from where you were standing. I guess she wanted us to know that she's OK." The light has not turned itself off or on since.

"There's A Man Standing at the Foot of the Bed!"

The roots of this story started several years before the final chapter. My husband would wake up in the middle of the night screaming at some man he was seeing or dreaming was standing at the foot of the bed. Once he even replied to my denial with, "Yes, he is! He's standing right there!" pointing to the footboard. I turned on the light and no one was there. This happened several times over about four years, always his seeing the man, not me. Then it stopped.

A year or more later, I woke up in the wee hours. I listened. My baby was not crying. Why was I awake? I had so many sleepless nights with her allergies and ear infections; I did not appreciate being awakened when she was sleeping. Her crib was in an adjoining room and as I looked in that direction I saw a man standing there. I squeezed my eyes closed and open several times, but the image never changed. I remembered what Sis, the psychic, had told me to do if I ever saw a ghost. Say (or think) "In the name of God, how can I help you?" In my head I was screaming it over and over while my heart raced and the image did not change.

Finally I calmed down long enough to listen to the logical side of my brain say, "If you don't shut up, how can you hear his answer?" So I quieted down. Then this wave of peace and calm washed over me, so comforting.

I heard, "You can't help me. I'm here to help you." It was so reassuring I did not want him to leave. It was quite possibly the most peaceful feeling I have ever experienced. I stayed awake until he finally vanished.

When I called Sis the next day, she said she thought I had seen one of my spirit guides. "No," she said, "It was one of your daughter's guides. Yes, that's it. I'm getting goose bumps." Goose bumps are one of Spirit's ways of giving us confirmation, she went on to explain. It was certainly a relief to know that despite my daughter's health concerns, there was a spiritual force watching over her, keeping her safe.

Not to Fear...

My experiences communicating with spirits and ghosts have left me with the sense that they are not to be feared. When I see how they are depicted in movies and TV, it irritates me and I usually whisper to the person sitting next to me, "They are not like that!" I have never seen a dismembered body or anything bloody or menacing. And perhaps that is because my guides choose to protect me from such things. I believe we can tell Spirit what is and what is not acceptable to us. For example, I have not been called upon to help the police in solving crimes, and I think that is to protect me from having to witness the trauma, even secondhand. I have done readings for people who have experienced some awful things and those things are not revealed in the session unless they are relevant to the subject matter we are covering that day. When I channel people who have died, if the manner of their deaths is not relevant to what they want to communicate to the loved ones left behind, they don't reveal it to me.

I have no reason to believe that your guides will not keep you as protected as mine do. That is what they are there for, after all. Call upon them. Pretty often people tell me they never see ghosts and they are perfectly happy that way. I tell them that is probably why they don't see them. Spirit cooperates with our intentions, as long as they are aligned with our highest good.

If You Want to See Ghosts

There is plenty of curiosity about ghosts, especially in today's media. Rare is the appearance of Elvis or Abe Lincoln, however, so it would help you not to set your expectations too high. Most of the time, in my experience, ghosts are the spirits of loved ones who have passed away, sometimes even relatives that you never met.

They will come to you if you call them, even if you don't see them. For me, I have to let go of the desire to "see" them with my two eyes and allow the image to appear, like an apparition floating in my peripheral vision. Pay attention to other psychic cues you may receive such as the person's name just pops into your mind, or you find yourself thinking about them. You can experience the presence of ghosts using the same psychic senses you use to receive intuitive messages.

If you apply the senses that you use to pick up psychic information, to the quest to experience a ghost, you will discover that sometimes you see them, sometimes you hear them, and sometimes you just know they are there. Sometimes there is an experience of a "chill" or a cold sensation, or goose bumps. And if you think about how you know someone has just walked up behind you even though they made no noise, you can refer to that same sensation to know that a spirit is with you.

Your guides are always with you, and if you want to experience their presence, ask them. I now own my dad's car and I often invite him to come along for a ride when I have the top down. Out of the corner of my eye, I can see him sitting there, always wearing his seat belt! He comes because I call him, and sometimes when he senses that I need him around, as does my Mom and other loved ones. I am certain that my family is not unique and that yours are around you as well.

In a Nutshell...

Your children have spirit guides and guardian angels just as you do. When your children say they have experienced the presence of a spirit, act very matter-of-factly. Don't make a big deal of it in either a negative or a positive way. I believe that all of us could see spirits and energy when we were first born and slowly we lost the ability. If your child still has it, gently encourage it. You might see if the early drawings of people done by your child include extra colors around the person that you cannot see – an orange line outside of their arm, a light blue halo. I have heard of children doing this, but my daughter who has very good aura vision, only did so when we asked her to "draw our colors."

If your child is frightened by a ghost, do whatever you would do if your child were frightened by something else. Most of what we fear is not real. We worry about the future, about things that never happen. We worry about things we perceive as dangerous, and our children are no different. When we are in the midst of fear, what we need is validation -- that is it okay to feel afraid -- and reassurance -- that despite our fear we are not alone.

It never hurts to say what I was taught, when you or your child encounter a spirit, "In the name of God, how can I help you?" Calling upon the name of God reminds you that the One Presence is infinitely powerful. Asking how you can be of service puts the emphasis on your own generosity. Many of the spirits I have encountered, as well as those you hear about, want help in going to the Light or want to be acknowledged in some way. My aunt who turned out the lights never reappeared in my house after we acknowledged her presence. And truly, isn't that what everyone wants – to be given acknowledgement, to be noticed?

Chapter Seven Exercises

1. Think back to your own childhood. Do you remember seeing ghosts or spirits? Jot down what you remember about it.

_____

_____

_____

2. Did you or have any of your children had an imaginary friend? Often children find that having an imaginary friend is more acceptable to their parents than seeing ghosts. What do you remember about your 'friend?' Did it have a name?

_____

_____

_____

3. What about your pets? Have you ever noticed them looking at something that you could not see? Going to the door before anyone is there? Showing dislike for someone when you could perceive no reason for it?

_____

_____

_____

4. Can you ever remember seeing a ghost that you thought might be one of your spirit guides or guardian angels? If you haven't and are feeling brave, invite your guide to communicate with you. Notice if a name pops into your head or you find yourself 'knowing' something you were not aware of previously.

_____

_____

_____

_____

5. If you have a loved one who has died, I am certain they have been around you, especially if you wanted them to be. The most prevalent sign of the spirit of a loved one being present is an unexpected smell. I know my mother is around when I can smell cigarette smoke when no one is smoking. My sister smells cinnamon when our grandmother is around. Phantom aromas I call them. Pay attention. Call upon a loved one and then notice what signs show up. Note them:

_____

_____

_____

_____

*Isn't that what everyone wants –
to be acknowledged,
to be noticed?*

8

Signs

Intuition is all about signs and messages and the interpretation of them. As discussed earlier, Spirit has its own language and part of the discernment is in learning to decipher it. In the hope that you will learn from my experience, I will share many of the signs that I have received both in and outside of readings, as well as signs I have known others to ascertain.

My Favorite Stories about Signs

The Bank Robber Story

Every time I think of this story, it brings a smile to my face. I was reading for a client who was trained in a profession that dealt with people in all levels of society. Her deceased father was communicating with her through me, and she inquired about her career. I channeled his message to her about how she would be helping people and directing them to additional sources of help. When she asked which types of people would be her clientele, he answered, "Not to worry. You won't be in any danger. It won't be people who have robbed banks or anything."

Before I could continue she sat up straight in her chair, raised her index finger and exclaimed, "That's it!" and began to laugh. At my confused expression she continued, "In my head I kept saying, 'Dad, if this is really you, make her say bank robber!' and he did!" We both got a hearty laugh, courtesy of her father. While the usage was slightly varied, the reference could not have been more specific.

"Well," I pointed to my recorder, "you have the proof on your CD." I went on to tell her how grateful I was that she didn't let me know that she was testing me because I find such things intimidating and feel that I don't do my best tuning in when I feel like I am under a microscope.

I encourage you to share the details when you are gathering information for someone else, even if the details seem insignificant; maybe especially if they seem insignificant. You may not know how much some small snippet of information might help reassure the other person or how significant it might be.

The Tea Bag

Once I was channeling a loved one for a family and while they were comforted by his words, they had not heard enough to completely convince them that it was indeed their husband and father who was speaking. As almost an afterthought at the end of the session, he made a joke to them. "Now don't throw away my tea bag!" he said. I described the old saucer I could see sitting on a shelf next to the kitchen window with a tea bag that had to be completely used up before it merited a place in the trashcan. It reminded me a lot of the one my grandfather used and I almost didn't mention it, but am so glad that I did.

"How could you possibly know about his tea bag?" they wondered aloud. They were visibly relieved that he provided this small detail as comfort, not only that he was indeed communicating with them, but also that he had not lost his sense of humor.

The Bird

I was reading for a woman who was distraught because she felt that her late husband was not reaching out to her from the other side, even though *I* could feel his presence very strongly and could tell that he was with her constantly. I asked him to give her a sign, a way to know that he was around. An image of a lone bird singing in a tree came to mind, followed by another image of gatherings of birds with one bird setting itself apart from the others. I explained to her that she could tell that he was reaching out to her especially when she heard one bird singing alone, quite clearly by itself.

Before I could continue, a bird landed outside the window and began singing very sweetly and quite loudly. I pointed to the source of the sound and we both smiled as I said, "kind-of like that!" I was impressed by his ability to send the sign at such an opportune time and told her so. There had never before or since been a bird at my window.

Signs on the Radio

I am embarrassed to admit this, but when I am desperate, I will play what I have come to know as Radio Karma. It all began when I was 15 and had just met my first boyfriend. My friend, Amy, and I had been roller-skating when Bob came over and asked me to join him in a couples skate. He later asked for my phone number and I was quite enamored with him. As we were getting into the car to go home that evening, my mother started the engine and the first song to play on the radio was

"Bobbie's Girl" which was not even close to being in the top-40 at that time.

Amy pointed to the radio and called out, "It's a sign!" It was! Bob became my first boyfriend and we dated for several months. And the experience with the sign started us along a path of asking for signs from the songs that played on the radio all through high school and beyond. We developed a system to avoid turning on the radio and catching only the last few words or notes of a song. "The next full song that plays on the radio will be a sign about..." and invariably it was about some guy who held our interest.

"Must've Been Love..."

So as a grown-up psychic, why would I need to use the radio as an intuitive tool? Spirit uses all sorts of avenues to communicate with us, why not the radio? Or the TV? Or a message found in any sort of media? I believe there are more signs than we realize, and *the trick to finding them is to look for them.*

My examples of signs on the radio would fill a book, but I would like to share just a couple more very accurate ones. The first involved a friend who was contemplating divorce. She did not want to disrupt her family's lives and cause any more pain than was being caused by the dysfunctional marriage, but she did not know how much longer she could stay in the awful limbo. She asked for a sign and got the song, "It Must Have Been Love, But It's Over Now." Not only did she feel a strong sense of peace that she was headed in the right direction, but a little comforted too that she and her husband had in fact loved each other, tried their best, and could no longer stay married. It might sound silly to find comfort in a song on the radio, but what harm does it cause?

"Heal Him"

This example looked like it was going to put me in an awkward situation. I had an acquaintance who was going to undergo surgery to remove a polyp. This man was very kind and generous and I highly regarded him, although I did not know him very well. We were both members of a group and attended regular planning meetings. He was to have his surgery the day after a meeting, which was about a week after I began to get messages. The first message told me in no uncertain terms, "Heal him." Inwardly I groaned. I hardly knew this man and the last thing I wanted to do was make him feel uncomfortable.

No one in the group knew about my spiritual work. I bargained with my guides, tried to talk them out of it, to be honest. "I want to help him, but I don't want to be considered weird," I told them. And I didn't want to make a fool of myself either. Several people in the group, I imagined, believed that spiritual healings were performed only by holy giants and not moms who repeatedly arrive late to meetings. I persisted in my resistance.

Finally I gave my guides one last opportunity to let me off the hook. I was driving to work listening to the radio. "If I am supposed to do this healing, it will be clear in the next song on the radio," I declared. Weak, I know. When the song came on at first I gave a sigh of relief. I knew this song and it wasn't about healing! But I had forgotten that one line until I heard it loud and clear, "You are my only medicine."

"OK, OK, I'll do it," I told my guides and then set about giving them my conditions. "If you want me to heal him, you are going to have to set up the situation where the two of us are alone together. And he must be open to it. I do NOT want to force this on him." I couldn't feel any resistance from my guides, so I believed we were on the same page.

That evening I sat at the meeting pondering my next step. I really wasn't paying much attention to the discussion when I heard a voice in my head say, "Heal him now."

Oh! I could do a distance healing from across the room where he would not even have to be aware of my actions. Whew! I continued to listen as the guides told me what to ask for and what to do. I imagined sending a beam of healing light into the area where the growth was and these words came to me, "When they go in to do the surgery tomorrow, there will be no polyp." It took less than a minute and I knew my work was done. I was relieved and certain that he had been healed.

Several days later I learned from another member of the group that our friend was doing well. "It was the strangest thing," she said, "when they went in to do the surgery, there was no polyp." She even used the same words I had been given!

Eventually, I got to know him better and told him what I had done. He was touched and a little embarrassed, and he thanked me. "You're welcome," I responded, "but I didn't heal you, God did. I was just the conduit."

License Plates

When I was newly pregnant with my first daughter, before the days of early pregnancy tests, I spent a month wondering. It was an unplanned blessed event and the timing could have been much better. Nevertheless, one afternoon as I was stopped at a traffic light pondering the possibility, a car pulled up next to me with the license plate MUM 629. I was shocked. I knew it was meant for me because my birthday is June 29th (although I was surprised to learn that God was British!).

My dad's birthday was July 29 and he sent me another sign via a license plate last week. We used to have constant conversations about convertibles and which one got the best gas mileage, which one looked the nicest, which was the most practical. I told him I really liked a certain model that I had test-driven but was unsure about its gas mileage and practicality. In a parking lot last month was that very model with the license plate 729 DAD. I feel like Dad was giving me his blessing to get whatever car I wanted, even though when he was alive he said he thought that model got poor gas mileage. In both cases, they were ordinary plates and not specially selected vanity ones.

Dimes

I have heard plenty of stories of people finding pennies after a loved one dies, "pennies from heaven," or other signs like birds, butterflies, or unique cloud formations. Both of my parents sent rainbows: my mother on the day of her funeral, and my dad several times since he has died, even when there was no rain in sight. My dad also sends dimes. When I found the first one on the day he died, I remembered that the vacation fund when we were growing up was comprised of a large jar of dimes and made the connection that the dime was a sign from my dad. I find them in the most unusual places and my friend Ruth even found one in a laundry load of towels.

After I received my father's car this spring, complete with an extra right front fender to replace a rusty one, we had an unfortunate encounter with a deer. The good news was that she dented the right front fender (the one I already had the replacement for); the bad news was that she also took out the flip-up headlight. A serendipitous series of events concluded with three very generous men (Russ, Matt, and Ian) actually delivering the replacement headlight to me from a distant city – *and then installing both the headlight and the fender at no charge!* I was overwhelmed with gratitude to them. As we were standing in the driveway talking afterward, Russ took off his shoe saying, "I've had something in my shoe since we left Denver!" He turned it upside down and a dime rolled onto the concrete. I knew my dad was pleased at my good fortune.

Our family has a joke that while we deeply appreciate the dimes and the message they convey, we would be really impressed if he could produce $100 bills! It appears he has upped the ante already. Just this week my daughter found a $10 bill in her toaster!

Answered Prayer

What this all really boils down to is answered prayer. We ask God/ the Universe/ Spirit to let us know that our loved ones are okay, to give us guidance and comfort us, and we receive encrypted messages in the form of signs. If you take any message from this book let it be this: *Ask! Ask! And ask some more!* People sit down to readings and their guides are champing at the bit to communicate with them, to receive instructions, and to help them in any way.

No prayer request is too small. I had to get a routine x-ray this week and really did not want to get the same nasty technician who had done it the last few times. I didn't realize that I had said a prayer about it until a new technician called my name and I knew it had been answered.

If you don't know what to pray for, ask for guidance. Another friend of mine was grieving the loss of a long-term relationship after her partner moved out of the home they shared. While she wanted to get married, he did not but still wanted a connection with her. In a moment of divine inspiration she asked, "God, if I am not supposed to be with him, please make me fall out of love with him." She woke up the next morning with a changed heart. Suddenly she could see flaws in the relationship that would continue to make them both unhappy, and she was truly no longer in love with him.

The universe is conspiring for your highest good whether you realize it or not. Sometimes we unwittingly fight against the flow because we think we know what is best for us. If you are swimming upstream, you know it. There is no shame in turning around and allowing the current to direct you to that nice sunny sandbar for a rest.

What If a Sign Is Wrong?

It happens. Everything seems to point one way, but then the opposite happens. This intuition business is not an exact science. I can keenly recall two instances when the information that I have received for clients was completely the opposite of the truth. On the other hand, two blatant examples in 25 years is not a bad average.

Sometimes people are given inaccurate information to steer them in the right direction. Your guides know the big picture, and they know what to tell you to move you toward your highest good. So when your guides direct you to go ahead and apply for a job, then you don't get it, it seems like they were wrong. Yet the preparation for the interview ends up being just what you needed when the ideal job opens up.

From our human perspective, we can never fully know the value of our experiences here on earth, but God knows. And God speaks to us in more ways than I can count, but certainly through our spirit guides and guardian angels. It is fruitless to focus on some piece of information that seemed to direct us to a conclusion that never came.

I can think of two separate clients who were single and looking for new relationships. Both of them were told that they had not fully let go of an old love but *if they would*, someone new was waiting in the wings. In each case, the women asked me for more information about the potential new love, and of course I shared what I saw. In both of their next readings, the new man had not materialized. They were almost accusatory in their response to this disappointment. I had been accurate in everything else I had told them, why not this, they wondered aloud. Upon further revelation, I could see each of them holding on to the idea of the old relationship "just in case." One of the ladies was told quite bluntly, "As long as you keep him as your back-up plan, you are not allowing your new relationship to manifest."

I could see the past-life connections, that they had both had several previous relationships with the men, which gave them the sense of an enduring bond. It saddens me to see them still alone in this lifetime in the almost 10 years since the first reading, and more so because they have been given information that might help them to move forward with their lives. They were both told variations of, "you can't jump in the boat while still holding on to the shore," yet they were unable to let go. It is difficult for me to witness my clients making decisions that do not serve them, especially repeatedly.

Other times, the information is flat-out wrong with no contingencies. I don't really have an explanation for it, but want to share one of my own.

Twins

When I was pregnant with my third daughter (the same one whose arrival was confirmed by the wee-hours message mentioned earlier) my psychic gifts were starting to kick into gear. Well, mostly. I was convinced that she was a boy (just as I was convinced that her two sisters were boys!). Since I was very healthy, there was never a sonogram. I saw a psychic midway through the pregnancy and she asked me if I were carrying twins. "I keep seeing twos," she remarked.

Some outward signs supported this idea, mainly that my belly was extended quite *outward*—much more so than my other pregnancies! If I needed to prepare for *two* more children instead of just one, I wanted as much advance notice as possible. I felt silly asking my doctor, so I went to a higher authority. I had heard of this technique called putting out the fleece, where you ask God for not one but three signs, based on a bible story where Gideon asks God for a sign then not believing it, asks for another and another. (Judges 6:36-40)

"OK, God," I silently prayed, "if I am carrying twins, please give me three signs in the next 24 hours." Before the evening was out, I cracked an egg that had two yolks and the Twins won the World Series. The next morning a local television show that I watched devoted its entire program to -- you guessed it -- twins! I was incredulous. At my next appointment I asked my doctor if it were possible and he assured me, no, there was just one big healthy baby, which turned out to be correct.

I have no explanation for how I received three such distinct signs that pointed to something that was not true. Maybe it just means that God has a sense of humor. And incidentally, there are two twos in her birth date!

In readings, when I receive information that is the opposite of what is true, I find I sometimes pick up on what my clients *want,* and they are holding such energy around it that it feels like it is fact. For example, I read for a woman once whose husband left her but I did not know that yet. I was having trouble picking up on the marriage situation and the guides wanted to provide insight for my client about one of her children instead of her husband. My client kept redirecting the reading back to her marriage and showed me a photo of a happy family gathering. I felt confused but told her it felt like her husband was committed to the marriage even though there was a doubt in the back of my mind that I couldn't quite figure out.

The client seemed pleased to have 'fooled' me into seeing the marriage as she wanted it rather than how it was. With the fog lifted, the guides provided a lot of additional information about the relationship, which my client was not interested in learning. To this day I am unsure why she wanted the reading in the first place, but I was disappointed that my information was off target. I had to let go and realize that everyone has bad days. I do not claim to be accurate all the time, and do the best I can.

Divination Tools – Cards, Pendulums, etc.

There are all sorts of tools available to help you gain answers. Not only are there many different types of tarot cards, there are also angel cards, spirit cards, animal cards, and many more. If you want to try a deck, I suggest you go to a store that has the decks open so you can look at the cards themselves and see if they feel comfortable for you. I have been given decks of cards that I have loved, and others that didn't fit me, which I passed along to someone else who felt drawn to them. Most decks come with a booklet to help you get started, and they can be quite fun to practice with.

People also use pendulums and other ancient tools such as the I-Ching to gather their answers. My thoughts on any sort of tool is to see how well it works for you, if it is helpful or not, and then use accordingly. I have found that a pendulum can be very accurate upon occasion for me and completely wrong in others, so I do not rely on them. I have found the tools that work best for me and focus mainly on my own intuition when reading for clients. However, when I want to gain information for people closest to me or myself, I will use automatic / channeled writing mainly, and the Mother Peace tarot deck upon occasion. Cards can bring out issues or ideas that I might overlook, or that are too close for me to see, and since the cards are outside of my head, I can look at them more objectively.

Again with the cards, it helps to record your information to see how it pans out in the future. I also like to do yearly readings for my clients where they shuffle the deck and then select one card per month for the upcoming year. Those simple readings can be uncanny in their accuracy.

All Signs Point To...Patience!

Whatever method you use to tune in, however, I suggest that you keep track of both *what* you learn and *how* you intuit it. You will discover that you are more accurate in some areas, less accurate in others. For me, I tell clients that if I give you a number, you can count on it (no pun intended!), but names are not always so precise.

Once you get a feel for your own channels and which ones work best for you, you can gain confidence in your own abilities and begin to expand them. I would suggest that you avoid "over asking," however. I have seen people (OK, I have done it myself upon occasion) who did not like the answers they were receiving so they asked again and again hoping they would change. Ask yourself: do you really want to know? And then accept what you get.

Recognize that things don't always happen as quickly as we might like, so a measure of patience helps as well.

In a Nutshell...

If you think about it a while, you will probably recall several examples of signs received throughout your life. The easiest – and surest -- way to see signs is to look for them! Notice coincidences and serendipity in your everyday round. Listen to words on the radio, pay attention to license plates and things you pass by but may not have noticed until now. I encourage you to be light-hearted about it. *It can be a lot of fun!*

Also pay attention to feelings you have. The first time I drove by my future husband's home, he was out mowing the lawn and I "had a feeling." I didn't know what it was, but it got my attention. Five years passed before we were introduced. The first time I drove through Kansas City on a cross-country vacation, I got an unmistakable 'feeling.' Again, I was unclear of the message, but knew that somehow that city would have significance in my life. There was even a rainbow over the road as we drove into town. We moved there two years later, and it had never been a consideration before the job transfer was offered. I have found it helps to mention your feelings to someone to allow you to validate your hunches.

You may choose to buy a special deck of cards, such as angel, fairy, crystal or animal cards. There are many available in bookstores and spiritually centered shops. Take your time to choose the one that 'speaks' to you. If you try a pendulum or other technique, give yourself time to become skilled in it and delay judgment of your results for a while.

Chapter Eight Exercises

1. Try to remember times when you have received signs. Once you start jotting them down, more will come to you.

_____

_____

_____

_____

2. Ask Spirit for signs, answers to questions. If you want, play Radio Karma. Note the questions you ask and the answers you receive. Try different tactics and see if the answers coincide.

_____

_____

_____

_____

3. Go to a bookstore or metaphysical store and explore the different divination tools. See if any of them speak to you. Make notes of your first 'readings' and the answers that come through.

_____

_____

_____

4. Try different techniques with your cards or other tools. For example, you can use a regular deck of cards and say, "A red card means yes, a black card means no" or "an even card means yes, an odd card means no." Take notes about the different methods and their accuracy.

_____

_____

_____

5. If you want to try a pendulum, you can use a pendant on a chain. It helps if the pendant is round or balanced. The method I like is to start the pendant (pendulum) swinging in a circle and then ask, "Please show me a yes." Note the direction that the motion switched to, for example back and forth or side-to-side. Then start it swinging in a circular motion and ask, "Please show me a no." See if the direction changes. Note how it works for you and the answers you receive. In a little while, try again and see if the directions are consistent for you each time. Jot down your questions and the answers you receive.

_____

_____

_____

_____

_____

*Spirit is
seeking to communicate
with you
in every moment.*

9
Who Are "They"?

People view the world through their own individual filters, according to the beliefs they were raised with and those they have come to know as adults. My perception of the voices that speak to and through me and where they originate is unique to me and based on my own interpretations. I encourage you to agree or disagree with me, as you choose. It is not my intention to promote any belief system, which is why I refer to a Higher Power in many different ways throughout this book – God, Universal Life Force, Spirit, Divinity, Infinite Source, the 'I Am' Presence, and so on.

The quick answer to the above question is that "they" are spirit guides, guardian angels, totem animals, and loved ones who have died. There is one power moving in and through every being living or 'dead.' We are each an expression of that power. Just as human beings can be separated into many different categories by gender, occupation, religion, nationality, etc., so can this power be differentiated when it manifests as pure spirit.

Angels

I recently conducted a session where I channeled individual angels to a group of people. When it was "Susan's" turn, I mentioned that I saw her late husband, but that I wanted to give her a message from her angel, not him. She was very disappointed and commented, "Oh, I thought he was an angel now." I went on to explain to

161

her that while he is definitely in spirit form, I specify an angel as a spirit that seems to be of a higher vibration and whom we have known from our human perspective as only in the spirit form. So while her husband may be acting from the angelic realm, I was seeking a spirit who has been with her as a guardian angel throughout her life.

My experience of their energy and appearance is what tells me when I am encountering an angel rather than another form of spirit. Usually they appear to me with wings, as a means of illustration, and sometimes they are *very large!* It amuses me when a very tiny person shows up for a reading surrounded by angels that reach to the ceiling – small but mighty!

When angels appear, there seems to be a levity around them. They expect to be taken seriously and given respect, while at the same time emitting an energy that can best be described as unconditional love. When your angels make themselves visible during a reading, they want you to know that you are being protected and guided, comforted and supported. Their message could be summed up as,

> *"We are the highest expression of Infinite Power that you would feel comfortable experiencing around you. While you know that you are One with the Power, you can feel it best when it is given in easily acceptable, angelic doses. So here we are to help you, to make you feel that you are not alone, to assist you in making choices, to let you know that you have support when it feels like the world is against you. WE ARE HERE FOR YOU."*

The very first being that I channeled when I began doing automatic writing was my guardian angel. Not only does she keep watch over me, she told me, but also she wants to help me in any way that I ask, just as your angels do. Occasionally I give her assignments (such as helping the man with the homburg go to the light) or ask her to look in on my children, knowing that she will always return to me. It's kind-of like a homing pigeon with supernatural powers!

Once when I was struggling to get my retail store off the ground, I sat in the empty store and asked for the angels to help me. Business was slow. I looked up and saw three huge white angels enter the back of my store (through the wall). They each went a different direction, as though they were shopping, and one of them even made the rain sticks tinkle while moving past them. Upon reaching me at the counter, they gave me this message: "You have been focusing on *sending out* loving energy from the store. You need to shift your attention to *draw in* the customers you need. Become a magnet so that people can come to you for what they need." They proceeded through the store and then vanished. Immediately, I did as they suggested and in the final two hours I was open that day, I put more sales on the cash register than I had in weeks. Customers seemed to come out of nowhere!

Fairies

Occasionally I have a client show up with fairies around them. Invariably when I mention this, they are not surprised. It is unclear why some people seem to have these tiny beings of light around them and others do not. Before I saw them for myself, I have to admit I considered them something entertaining out of Peter Pan, but certainly not fodder for a serious psychic reading. That changed when I had a profound experience with fairies that helped me a great deal.

I had started a load of laundry before going to bed one night. I woke up a short while later and saw these three lights dancing in my room. At first I looked to see if there could be some practical explanation for them, but I keep my room very dark at night and no light was coming in from outside. For a while I watched them zip and zoom near the doorway to the room until I was more alert than asleep. I figured I might as well go to the bathroom while I was awake, which I did. On my way back to bed I heard water running and it sounded peculiar. I went down to check and found my washing machine overflowing. The shut-off valve had malfunctioned.

Not only was the main floor filling with water, but it was also running through the floor into the basement. I shut it off and began a long cleanup process. While there was a huge mess, I cannot imagine how bad the damage might have been if the fairies had not awakened me and it had continued until morning.

So now when I see fairies around someone I know they are watched over and often being given the message to lighten up, "don't take things so seriously!" Fairies seek to remind us to be light-hearted, joyful. Imagine how much fun it would be to have wings and be able to fly!

Spirit Guides

While angels and fairies provide guidance and insight, I find that spirit guides get down in the trenches with us. They help you meet the deadlines and balance the budget. It is not unusual for people to have several different guides that perform different duties – one gives business advice, another parenting tips, still another helpful information for dealing with your difficult friend. They can be highly entertaining as well.

When I did my first automatic writing, three of my guides showed up the first evening. Since then I have become aware of several more. Sometimes one will show up to help me through a difficult time and then fade away as my need diminishes.

Clients are interested in the names of their guides, and this often surprises the guides who seem to view their names as unimportant. Unless there is some significance to the name itself, such as the meaning of the name is relevant (for example, Ann means grace), they are more concerned that the client has a way to contact them than what the name actually is. Once I actually had a spirit guide tell me to make up a name for him. I suggested the first name that popped into my head and he said, "OK, let's go with that!"

What seems most important to spirit guides is that we know they are with us, they are watching over us, and they want to help us.

They are with us.

Before we come into a human life, we are pure spirit surrounded by other loving spiritual beings. I see it as a momentous occasion with great fanfare. "Lance has decided to have a human experience! What a brave soul! Let's all rejoice and support him as best we can!" And then they line up, volunteering to be your spirit guides, guardian angels, telling you they will come in as your little brother or your wife. Before we venture into an incarnation, we are immersed in unconditional love, given as much direction and support as possible.

As babies, we can often see the spirits and angels around us, and we recognize them. I love to observe babies looking around at the world, and wish they could tell us what they see. By the time we learn how to speak, the reality of the human existence has gradually eased out the awareness of the spiritual, and we forget who we are. Instead we focus our attention on acclimating to the human condition, meeting the developmental milestones expected of us.

Yet you may remember having an Invisible Friend when you were a child. Mine was named Peter and I even named Petey my pet rabbit after him. Peter and I would play on the swing set and have a splendid time, although he was not very good at pushing me to make me go higher. As I grew up, he faded from my experience and it wasn't until I started tuning into spiritual things as an adult that I understood who Peter was. I suppose he was a childhood guide because he has not reappeared to me.

They are watching over us.

Shortly after I began my automatic writing, our family planned to move across the country. On the night the moving van left the driveway with my car and all my earthly belongings (except what I had in a suitcase), I felt very alone. I had borrowed my grandfather's car to use until it was time to fly to our new home. I got inside and when I turned to back it out of the driveway, I realized I was actually in good company. I gasped a little at the sight, but in the back seat, shoulder to shoulder, sat three of my spirit guides, the same three who spoke to me on that first night, just weeks before. If I hadn't been feeling so sad, it would have been comical, like my Three Musketeers packed into the backseat of a Chevrolet.

I have heard countless versions of people saved from harm's way in manners that defied the laws of physics. I cannot explain why sometimes our guides and angels intervene on our behalf and other times they do not, why sometimes we need to ask for help and others it seems to fall straight from heaven to our doorstep. The prudent path, I believe, would be to ask for help and hope to get it rather than give up before you even get started.

They want to help us.

There is energy around the act of asking for what you want and making plans. Repeatedly, I find peoples' guides asking, "What do you want?" In speaking our intentions aloud, it creates a charge around them, gives them wings, so to speak, "from your lips to God's ears." God is always listening, so decide what you want and ask for it. *Don't be afraid that you don't deserve good things or better things.* There is no miserly being in the ethers saying, "Why you little ingrate! So you think you deserve more, do you? I'll just take from you what little you have!" No, I believe the Presence wants us to have all good things and that we limit how much we have by how comfortable we are with it. It does help to be grateful, though, for what we do have. An attitude of gratitude creates an energy field that draws to us more and more good.

"How good can you stand it?"

My friend Mary Ann taught me this game years ago, and I play it on occasion. Since we all have as much as we can stand, ask yourself, 'how good can I stand it?' When you are falling asleep at night, in that space between awake and asleep, let your imagination have a little fun. Start wherever you like – tangible things like houses and cars, or intangible things like relationships – and picture the very best that you could tolerate. You might find that you really could not handle having a 14-bedroom mansion with a staff of 20, but you could accept a slightly larger home with a nice backyard. Spirit gives you Carte Blanche when it comes to your heart's desires, so dream big!

I had two funny, revealing experiences with this game that taught me just how little goodness I could accept. In the one, I was visualizing a new windshield for my 13-year-old van. Not a brand-new van, mind you, but just a new windshield. When I realized how much I was willing to limit the prosperity flowing into my life, I had to laugh at myself. Of course I deserved a new vehicle (even two!) but I had to shift my comfort level first.

It is important to realize that when you accept abundance into your life, you do not take it from someone else. As Sis, my first mentor told me, "There is plenty out there. Take your share." And you get to decide how large of a share you deserve. Spirit says there is no limit.

The second ah-ha moment with the game actually was a gentle nudge from my guides while I was playing. "A massage once a week," I decided. "Yes, I could stand to get a wonderful, relaxing massage once a week."

A voice interrupted my thoughts, "If that is true, then why is there a gift certificate for a massage sitting on your dresser *that has been there for six months?*" Good question. Maybe I wasn't quite as open to prosperity as I wanted to be, but the path was becoming clearer.

Totem Animals

Native cultures seem more in tune to animal spirit guides than other more 'modernized' ones. In general, native cultures focus on nature whether animal, vegetable, or mineral, so it follows that their spirituality will be centered on those things as well. I encourage you to explore the wealth of wisdom available on those topics, and to Google "(your specific animal) totem" to find out what the lore is around them.

Once you begin to consider that perhaps a spirit animal (or several) are around to assist you, the identity of that animal will quickly become evident. Think about animals you see regularly and then look up the meaning of them. For example, if you always see rabbits on your way to work, be aware of an energy of fertility or prosperity in your job.

I led a Spirit Guides meditation several years ago with some teenagers I found hanging around my house, a few of them related to me. One of the crowd really was not interested in the meditation but didn't want to be left out, so he joined us. "Brad" considered himself an atheist, and thought he was humoring the rest of us by participating. In our post-meditation discussion, he said, "All I saw was a polar bear. It didn't really seem to have a message for me, though." Several of his friends pointed out that the bear was likely one of his totem animals/ spirit guides, and he shrugged.

A few weeks later I ran into his father who is a friend of mine. "Did you know Brad saw a bear on the way home from your house the other night?" he asked me. "It was just a couple streets from our house. He turned his car so the bear was lit by the headlights." So convinced was Brad that he saw a bear cub in his wooded, suburban neighborhood that his parents almost called animal control. I believe his seeing the bear was a confirmation of his totem animal.

Really big animals

More than one person has told me of having a vision of a giant version of their spirit totem. We pay more attention to things that are extraordinary than if the animal had appeared right-sized, and that is why I think they show up that way. The human-sized bird at the side of the road has a message for you, so pay attention. As with all messages from spirit, notice the trigger (seeing the animal) then what happens immediately afterward to discern what the message may be.

Deceased animals

Often the beloved pets we once had will visit us as spirits. We had a Great Dane when I was growing up and he visits me occasionally. I was surprised the first time he appeared while I was receiving a massage, but have come to know that this precious black dog wants me to know he is watching over me. Many of my clients tell me of being visited by their pets who have died, and it seems pretty commonplace.

Mostly, the message that accompanies our deceased pets is one of comfort. They know how much their presence meant to us when they were 'alive,' and they want to offer that unconditional love to us again.

Deceased Loved Ones

One of the most comforting things to experience after a loved one dies is feeling like they are still with us, just in a different form. A dear friend just lost her husband and the night after he died she heard him calling her name. She knew it was his way of letting her know he wasn't so far away.

How do we know it's really them?

Why would it *not* be them? Some people are afraid that it is their own imagination creating something that they want so badly to experience. Our imaginations are connected to Spirit, so maybe they are actually a channel to receive information rather than a contradiction to it. What is the harm in believing that your loved one is reaching out from the other side to communicate with you? Now if the message tells you to drive the wrong way down the expressway, please reconsider, because no one on the other side – spirit guide, angel, or deceased loved one – would ever direct you to do something that would cause harm to you or anyone else.

They send signs.

In readings clients often ask me how they will know when their loved one is trying to communicate with them. The answer is along the same lines as the directions for tuning in to psychic information: *trust it and ask.* Shortly before he died, my dad and I were watching two cardinals playing in the trees. He even asked me to take a photo of them, which I did. Now when I see a pair of cardinals, I feel like he is saying hello. Undoubtedly, there will be similar signs from your loved ones – a song, an animal, a certain model of car, even a commercial on TV.

It is a privilege for me to offer a link for clients to their loved ones on the other side, especially when they feel reluctant to trust that the rainbows are signs and not just what the sky does when the sun shines through the rain. During a reading once, a woman was missing her deceased brother very much, and I could tell that he was around her a great deal. While she had acknowledged many of the messages he had sent her, there was another he wanted me to point out.

He showed me a vignette of her kitchen, first little puddles of water on the floor, and then an image of himself tapping the ice dispenser on the front of her refrigerator, releasing just one cube at a time. "Have you been finding tiny puddles of water on your kitchen floor?" I asked her.

She looked incredulous. "Yes! And I can't imagine where they are coming from!"

I explained what her brother had shown me and she laughed out loud. "He was always playing little jokes on me," she chuckled.

They send aromas.

Studies have shown that the sense of smell is the one most keenly tied to our memories, so it makes 'sense' that our loved ones would tap into our memories by producing aromas that remind us of them. My dad told a story of smelling cigar smoke in his strictly no-smoking-allowed house, and then coming across a memento from his uncle Henry. You guessed it. Henry smoked cigars.

Don't be surprised if no one but you can smell it. That seems to be part of the joke for them. When my mother wants to get the family's attention, she'll make the cigarette smell so strong that several of us can smell it, but not all.

They are with you and they can hear you.

Please believe me, your loved ones are around you. All you need do is think about them, and they are listening. And don't worry or feel embarrassed that they are watching your every move. They come from a place of deep compassion, and they remember what it was like to have the limits of a human existence. I have never known a spirit to sit in judgment of someone; they show only understanding and empathy. Even more than you can, they see all the factors influencing your life and your choices. They hurt with you, they laugh with you, and they cry with you. With you, not against you.

And, yes, they change.

Your late Aunt Gertrude was the most judgmental, narrow-minded person you ever knew? Not anymore! Once they cross over, they are no longer bound by the constrictions of their former personalities. So their inherent goodness (God-ness) is finally allowed to shine. Last week I channeled my client's mother who suffered from mental illness. While at first it was hard for my client to believe that it was indeed her mother speaking with such clarity and wisdom, the mother used enough personal references to make herself known. "It's strange to hear my mother now," she said. "She's so enlightened!"

My own mother has gone through such a metamorphosis she barely resembles her former beer-drinking, burp-out-loud self! If I had not watched her transform for my benefit, it would have been more difficult to understand. She keeps enough of her former personality traits in her communications to reassure me that it was, indeed, my very dogmatic mother helping me to do Reiki on a client.

So if your loved one on the other side does not seem exactly like the person you knew, please realize that your experience of them was from a human perspective. In Spirit they, like you, are One with All That Is. They are in their most pure form now and no longer bound by human limitations. So often when I first began channeling "dead people" they would chuckle and say that our perception is skewed. They didn't die! They were set free!

What Happens When Someone Dies

So what exactly does happen after we take that last breath? I have personally been present at two deaths, but feel like I have witnessed hundreds from the other (spirit) side. The dying process usually begins long before that last breath. While these examples do not apply in every situation, they are quite common.

They start to talk and think about dying.

It may sound cliché, but in the months before they die even completely healthy people start to talk about dying, or its inevitability. They may have dreams. Their family members may have dreams. About a year before my father died when he was still very healthy, both my brother and I dreamed *on the same night* that our dad died. Within a month, four other family members also dreamed of his death, although the details were different in each dream. I wrestled initially with whether or not to tell my dad of my dream, but opted to share it with him. It was a very emotional conversation, the first of many.

They do things they have always wanted to do, or have never done before.

I am sure you know of people who tied up loose ends or made an amends to someone before they died ~ even if their death was sudden and unexpected. There is a part of us that knows the completion is near, whether or not we are conscious of it. We joked when my dad helped with Thanksgiving dinner last year that "the end must be near, Dad is cooking!" We have several photos of him chopping vegetables and rolling out dough.

They discuss conversations they had with people who have died.

A friend's mother told her that she had seen "the baby," referring to a child she had delivered 40 years earlier who died shortly after birth. The mother was beaming with joy at finally seeing her child again, and what startled my friend was how matter-of-fact her mother was about it.

As my grandfather was grieving the loss of his wife of 59 years, my sister brought him an Irish Setter dog to help ease his pain. His health was failing and a few days later he told my sister, "Oh, I talked to your grandma today.

She said to enjoy the red dog, it's not your time yet." He was never one to speak of anything metaphysical, but the conversation was so real to him he was unafraid. It was a few weeks later that he died.

They hear you right up until the end.

A neighbor of mine was dying of lung cancer last year and I would visit him on my walks several times a week. When he was put in a nursing home for his last few days, I went to see him. He was considered unresponsive, but I knew "he was still in there." As I reassured him that wonderful things awaited him, and thanked him for his friendship, a single tear rolled down his cheek as he held my hand tightly.

As my father lay dying, I sang to him. He had not opened his eyes in hours, and his breathing was labored. His mother came to me in spirit and suggested that I sing a lullaby that she had sung to him. When I started the "Hush little baby don't say a word," his eyebrows shot up and I could tell he was surprised and liked the song choice.

The final moments

If you have the privilege of being present as someone exits from this human world, I congratulate you. It is truly an honor. As I mentioned earlier, it takes a very strong soul to leave while surrounded by loved ones. How many times have you heard stories of people dying as soon as their family went to dinner or left the room for a short break? It is difficult to let go, especially when the loved ones are holding on, and so much easier to "sneak out the back door when no one is looking!"

The stories about the actual transition are very similar from one 'person' to the next. A magnet of pure, unconditional love pulls them into a space of wonder and bliss. Usually many loved ones are there, celebrating the reunion. There does not seem to be any lag time, just a smooth easy transition from being a spirit having a human experience to being a free spirit.

Where do they go?

The best explanation of the 'where' is that there is no explanation. There is neither time nor space in the spiritual, infinite world. It is very difficult for the human mind to grasp, so I suggest you let it go. I am confident that I will find out what I need to know, when I need to know it. Meanwhile, my work with Spirit points toward some understanding. Since there is no space, 'they' can be everywhere. And since there is no time, they can be everywhere all at the same time. Which means that I can channel your beloved great-grandmother, even if you are convinced that she has reincarnated as your niece, because I channel the part of her that is spirit.

Your infinite self is always in spirit. Your infinite, Higher Self still has all the same qualities it had before you came into this human experience; only now you are filtering your consciousness through a human mind. You are still One with All That Is, just as all beings are. Remember, what you focus on increases. So if you focus on your limited humanness, your concept of life will be centered on limitation. If you focus on your unlimited spiritual self, your experiences will be beyond your wildest dreams – infinite!

In a Nutshell...

We've taken a look at my concept of angels, fairies, spirit guides, totem animals and deceased loved ones. *It matters less* what *you call them than that you* call upon *them.* Whether the spirit who appears to you seems to have an ethereal quality (angel), a playful delight (fairy), a matter-of-fact sense of wanting to give you direction (spirit guides), seems to be an animal (totem animal), or feels like someone you once knew who has passed away (deceased loved one), I encourage you to communicate with them. Ask questions, listen and observe for answers. I do not subscribe to the idea that some spirits might seek to harm you, unless that is what you are seeking. *What you look for, you find.* We are surrounded by spirit in so many forms whose singular purpose is to help us in any way they can.

When you encounter a deceased loved one, or think you might have, I encourage you to pay particular attention. They will likely try to present some sort of evidence to let you know it's really them, whether signs or aromas. If in doubt, try believing it is truly the 'person' you suspect and see what happens. Don't be surprised if they seem different somehow. They have let go of the human conditions that limited them and are now free in spirit. Remember, this is a process for you of trying new things to see how they work. *Be selective when choosing with whom to share your experience.* Surround yourself with loving, supportive people and not naysayers who might take a pot shot at your self-esteem.

If you are preparing yourself for the death of a loved one, or even yourself, please keep in mind that it is a natural, normal process that each of us will experience eventually.

People preparing for their transitions back into spirit might begin to talk about death or do things they have never done before to make the most of their remaining earth time. As death draws nearer, you may notice them referencing conversations with people who have died or seeing angels or lights around them. My best interpretation of what happens after they die is that they float into a space where they are surrounded by the energy field of pure love, and specifically by those loved ones on the other side who have been waiting for them. It is joyful, peaceful, and celebratory. Consistently when I channel beings after they have died they struggle to find words to describe how peaceful and beautiful it is where they are.

Chapter Nine Exercises

1. Have you ever seen or experienced the presence of an angel? Jot down what you remember about the experience.

_____

_____

_____

_____

_____

2. What about fairies? If not, invite them to visit you and then see what happens! Note your impressions.

_____

_____

_____

_____

3. Who are your Spirit Guides? Can you see how each plays a different role in helping you?

_____

_____

_____

_____

4. Did you have an Invisible Friend while growing up?

_____

_____

5. Imagine you might have a Totem Animal. What might it be? Check on the Internet for more information about your animal spirit guide and write it down.

_____

_____

_____

6. Have you ever had a deceased loved one visit you? Did you receive any messages during the experience? Consider inviting one to visit you right now.

_____

_____

_____

7. Have you ever been present when someone died? What can you remember about the experience?

_____

_____

_____

_____

*Surround yourself
with loving,
supportive people.*

10
In Practice

As you get ready to embark on your new Highly Intuitive Life, or at least have the opportunity to apply some of these ideas in your daily round, I want to give you an understanding about how my intuitive and healing practice works.

My Three Agreements

As I worked out my own methods for doing psychic and healing work, my reliance on my own and others' spirit guides became clear. "We" had more than one discussion that revolved around my maintaining my own integrity and emotional safety while embarking on this adventure. While I rely completely upon Spirit for the message, the energy, and the interpretation of it, I came to realize that there were three principles pervading my work, our "deals."

1. Don't give me any information that I can't share.

People sometimes worry that I might withhold information that I don't think is in their best interest to know. I firmly believe that Spirit would never provide any information that is not aligned with the highest good of my clients. Rather than find myself in the position of deciding whether or not someone can handle certain information that comes up during a reading, I trust Spirit to do the editing and filtering. I am committed to sharing any information that comes through for my clients.

That's not to say that I don't ask clients from time to time if they "really want to know." For example, if I am being shown information about the timing of a loved one's death, I confirm that the client does indeed want to be privy to such information. You would think that I would stop this practice, since I cannot recall a single time when my client has declined information offered in that situation, but I want to make it clear that I honor people's right to choose.

2. I don't have to remember the details.

Since the information I receive in my readings is channeled directly from Spirit, it doesn't come from my conscious mind. After a reading is over, it leaves my short-term memory and I simply don't remember most of what was said. This is beneficial to my clients especially in subsequent readings because, since I don't recall the details of the previous reading, if information comes up again, it is because Spirit deems it important.

I think my clients appreciate that when they leave a session, almost all of the information leaves with them, which gives them a sense of privacy. On the other hand, I think they can experience some disappointment when they come for the next session and receive a blank stare from me when they say, "Remember when you told me...?" Sorry, but I don't remember. People who observe me during and after readings have told me that I appear in an altered state of mind and I can confirm this. While I am fully cognizant of what is going on and what is being said, there are parts of my brain that seem to be on vacation, namely those parts that handle details like how to work my recording machine or do math.

3. Give me only the information that I need to help my clients.

I don't need to know all the private details of my clients' lives. I want to provide helpful, practical information to assist and support them, and still honor their right to privacy. My agreement with Spirit is that peoples' lives are sacred and my role is to help them along their paths, and not necessarily know all the particulars. I feel most helpful that I can see only the portion that Spirit reveals to me.

When I first started reading, I had this client who appeared to me as a very tenderhearted and sensitive man who often cried during our sessions. We met several times and at the last one right before I moved out of state, Spirit revealed to me a large, dense energy field around him. When we talked about it, he shared that he was amazed that I had never seen it before, and that most psychics have trouble getting past the field to get an accurate reading for him. I wonder if Spirit kept it hidden from me because, well, it looked kind-of scary! Since I already knew his most innocent and vulnerable self, when I finally saw the shadow energy around him I found it informative, rather than frightening. He kept people at a distance because he didn't feel safe allowing them in.

There are probably dozens of other agreements that I have developed in the course of my psychic career. It boils down to my guides keeping me safe emotionally and psychically, while providing me with what I need to be of maximum service to my clients and students.

Karma

Several years ago a Native American healer told me that we humans have had so many past lives that every person we now encounter has some karmic connection to us. That means that the clerk at the grocery store may have delivered a telegram for you a few lives back, or even been in your class at the one-room schoolhouse. We are all connected, some of us more so than others. In other words, we all have some sort of karma with one another. I describe karma as a past-life connection and, like all connections, some are stronger and more compelling than others.

Almost everyone can describe an incident where upon meeting someone they felt like they had known this person forever. Their past-life encounters were likely frequent and significant. In one lifetime they may have been siblings, in another parent-child or husband-wife. We tend to reincarnate with the same group of souls, and sometimes we repeat the unfinished dramas; other times we correct them. I have a handful of clients that I know were relatives or close friends of mine in past lives. When they come for readings, we have this sense of "coming home." If you stop and think about it for a while, I'm sure you will be able to come up with names of people in your life who have always felt like they belonged with you.

What about negative karma?

Often I talk to people who presume that if they have "karma" with someone, it means they are "supposed to be together." Karma can indicate unfinished business, an energy or pattern from a past lifetime that was left unresolved for one reason or another, perhaps one of them died or circumstances separated them. I have seen people at odds with one another in present day, each one attempting to even an indeterminate score from other incarnations, which can perpetuate indefinitely. Until it is pointed out to them, it creates a vicious cycle in their lives that feels oddly reminiscent and familiar.

"Cheryl" had a tempestuous relationship with her husband, yet was unwilling to divorce him. In fact, when he asked for a separation, she clung to him desperately. When it was revealed in a reading that the two of them had been one-upping each other for lifetimes, she realized that while the ongoing battles were familiar, neither of them was served by trying to best the other. The awareness of karmic energy between them, almost from their very first date, opened the door to a greater self-awareness. She had a false feeling of wholeness while engaged in 'battle,' which blocked a sense of genuine self worth. Arguing with her husband energized her, made her feel alive, she realized, but at the expense of her peace of mind.

In Cheryl's case, they went on to divorce and, because they ended the cycle, have an almost amicable relationship for the benefit of their children. I have seen it happen more than once, though, where the couple were able to stay together and work through their differences once they identified the karmic patterns they were repeating.

There are no karmic 'victims'

There are people who view themselves as victims of life, and find the 'victim' pattern repeating in every relationship, in every job, all through their lives. It is unfortunate, to say the least. If you have a loved one who has the victim mentality, please realize that *you cannot change them.* While we would love to see that next boss or relationship be the one of their dreams, chances are it won't be until they decide to make some changes.

We all have an energy field around us that attracts and repels according to our core beliefs. What and whom you have in your life right now are the results of your thoughts up to this moment. *"What we think about, we bring about."* When people have a victim mentality, they expect bad things to happen to them, and can justify their belief by reciting at length all the horrible things dealt by the hand of fate. Pretty often they will even argue to defend their position, "Everyone is against me!" Part of their game can be to draw in people as 'rescuers', and then show how even the rescuer's heroic efforts are thwarted. Pray for them and let them go. When they are truly ready to change, help will come from seen and unseen places to support their choosing a new direction.

Meanwhile, it seems the most helpful thing we can do is stay out of their way, and stand in a neutral space. Neutrality is a powerful place to be. It is non-judgmental and requires no action or statement. That's not to say that we should be cold or uncaring. One of the most powerful things we can do for loved ones is to validate what they are feeling and acknowledge their right to have whatever emotion is presenting itself. Sorting out for yourself the difference between validation and getting caught up in their drama will empower you to maintain your own neutrality – and your own serenity.

A dose of compassionate understanding will go a long way, too. People who view themselves as victims probably have had a string of bad things happen to them, most likely in their past lives as well. There is a lot of evidence in their world to support their viewpoint. What they don't understand (and it can be difficult to see when you're dodging bullets) is that they do have some control in their lives. People have overcome insurmountable odds and do so every day. Establishing yourself in a position of loving, nonjudgmental support is probably the most helpful thing you can do.

Yesterday I had a client who was baffled that all of her relationships ended the same way -- he left her for another woman. She realized that in her subconscious she was somehow recreating this pattern in her life, but she lacked the understanding it took to change it. Her guides showed her a number of factors that were present in her life. First, she was not currently ready for Mr. Right, or even Mr. RightNow. Her children and her career were her priorities, even though her loneliness drove her to keep searching for her ideal partner.

But readiness, or lack thereof, was not the only factor. As her guides pointed out through the reading, she kept unconsciously setting up the situation so that she was abandoned. This awareness paved the way for a deeper understanding of her childhood and how her view of the world was established by her relationship with her parents, who emotionally abandoned her for other children and other interests. She was not a priority for them, she realized, and so she did not expect to be a priority in her dating and marriage relationships. It was further revealed that she had some significant abandonment experiences in past lives, which solidified the expectation in her present day experience.

The past-life realization provided the opportunity for a turning point. She could continue to repeat a destructive pattern, or she could change it. It seemed evident to me that she was ready to change it, or it would not have come up in the reading. Professional counseling was recommended for her, as well as plenty of introspective work like journaling and meditation.

Chakras

Entire books have been written about the energy centers believed in Eastern traditions to represent different aspects of our physical and spiritual bodies, and I encourage you to explore them if that is your interest. For our purposes, though, I think a brief overview of chakras is helpful to aid in understanding and meditation. Once you have a basic knowledge of where the energy centers are located and what their colors are, you can mentally explore them and meditate on them as well.

My guides have shown me that our auric fields are really more of a rainbow than a line of disconnected spots, with the colors being true at the chakra centers and then blending into combinations between them, just as they do in the sky courtesy of Mother Nature. Chakras appear to me as plates or disks revolving on a common axis that extends from the top of our heads straight through our bodies to our tailbones. "Aligning" the chakras describes a process where you visualize all of the disks stacked above and below each other, in a straight line. "Clearing" them involves releasing any stagnant or discordant energy that may be lingering or lodged there.

Color	Name of Chakra	Area in Body	Energy Present	Emotions (Pos/Neg)
Purple or White	Crown	Crown, top of head	Spirituality	Peace / Anger
Indigo bluish purple	Third Eye	Center of head behind forehead	Spiritual vision, psychic sight	Clarity / Anger
Blue	Throat	Neck	Communication, expressing our truth	Calm, Open / Anger
Green	Heart	Chest	Affection, love	Joy / Sorrow
Yellow	Solar plexus	Abdomen gut	Self-esteem, self-identity	Courage / Fear
Orange	Sacral	Pelvis below navel	Sexuality, creativity	Dignity / Shame
Red	Root	Tailbone	Physical body, humanness	Pride / Shame

There is also an energy shift that happens from one chakra to another, starting with the root chakra (red) at the tailbone, which represents our human bodies, and going through a metamorphosis to the crown chakra (purple or white) at the top of the head, which represents our spiritual selves. When the energy moves freely from one chakra to another, we feel peaceful and clear.

A Closer Look at Chakras & Emotional Centers

It took me a while to be able to relate the chakra chart to the emotions chart in Chapter 5, but Spirit was patient with me until I understood.

Anger

The top three chakras relate to our connection with spirit, our vision, and our ability to speak our truth. When any of those are blocked, our natural response is anger. Notice how stress (a polite word for anger) can result when we feel cut off from Spirit, or when we cannot see truth clearly, or when someone is discounting our vision, or when we cannot or don't feel safe in speaking our truth. In short, when energy cannot flow freely through any of the top three chakras, we can feel angry.

Sadness

It is easy to connect the feeling of sadness with an energy block at the heart chakra. When we feel a loss of love, our hearts actually ache; we can feel pain and discomfort in the center of the chest. I knew someone once who went to the ER because his pain over the rejection he was experiencing from his children was so acute; he thought he was having a heart attack.

Fear

The solar plexus chakra is all about feeling comfortable in our own skin, feeling accepted with a healthy level of self-esteem. When we feel disapproval, or even anticipate it, we feel fear. When you trace fear to its roots, you usually end up somewhere near 'aloneness' like we discussed in Chapter 1. The solar plexus chakra, when clear and open, allows us to feel a sense of "all is well."

Shame

The connection between the lowest two chakras and shame is fairly easy to see. Our society, despite recent changes, still attaches a lot of shame to sexuality, which is related to the sacral chakra. When you consider all the negative words that are synonyms for promiscuous, you get the idea. As for the root chakra and our human bodies, many of us in our religious upbringings were taught that we were "only human," and that we would only reach perfection when we died and "became one with God." Our humanness, instead of being celebrated as the journey we have chosen, was considered a source of shame. When you truly grasp that you are Spirit having a human life, then you will celebrate your humanness and no longer feel ashamed of it.

Energy Work

As I was developing my intuitive abilities, other psychics I knew introduced me to energy work, also called energy healing. The prospect of facilitating healing for someone else or even myself was exciting and I read several books on the topic. Gradually I began to practice various techniques that I learned.

My first 'success' happened when my friend, John, had a kidney stone. At the same time, I was having pain from an ovarian cyst and decided to try a technique to relieve my pain. I was in bed for the night and usually meditate before I go to sleep. Instead of meditating, on this Tuesday evening, I visualized healing energy in the form of white light surrounding and engulfing the cyst. In a very short time, the pain was gone and I could sense a large amount of energy still present at my disposal. I thought of John and the intense pain he had been experiencing and decided to send the energy to him, to heal his kidney stone. I happened to glance at the clock and it was 11 pm. I spent some time picturing the healing energy enveloping the stone, dissolving it, and relieving his pain. Eventually I went to sleep and forgot about it the next morning.

A few days later I ran into John and inquired about his pain. "It was the weirdest thing," he told me. "At around 11 o'clock on Tuesday night, it just went away completely, and has not returned." Then I remembered the visualization I had done and told him about it. He thanked me and we both marveled at the incredible power of Spirit.

Since that incident I have been privileged to participate in several healings and have witnessed my efforts assist in the disappearance of two tumors or cysts, as well as many other positive results. I have also become a Reiki Master and a Oneness Blessing Giver, and teach healing techniques whenever given the opportunity. Here's a brief overview of my understanding of energy work.

What is Energy Work?

Whenever people choose to be conduits for healing energy, they are doing energy work.

Where Does the Energy Come From?

An energy worker (anyone who wants to facilitate healing) taps into the energy Source of the Universe – God, Universal Life Force, Prana, the One Presence, or any of its many names. This Source is always present, always available, always focused on good.

How Do You Tap Into It?

It's all about intention. The Source is always there, waiting to be called upon. Setting the intention to channel healing energy is the first step to set it in motion. Then, listen to your inner guidance and follow the directions you receive to keep yourself in the flow.

There are many different "brands" of healing practice, and each has its own techniques for tapping in. I believe it all boils down to asking Spirit, even just intending it without using specific words.

How Does a Healing Work?

Usually 3 elements are needed for energy work:

1. Source	2. Channel or "healer"	3. Receiver
Always present	Sets the intention; Allows energy to flow through	Accepts the energy; Receives the healing

1. Source We have already established that Spirit is omnipresent, so there is no need to worry whether or not the power is there for the healing to work. It is.

2. Channel or 'healer' Imagine that Spirit is like electricity. While it is always flowing through your house, you cannot use it without tapping into it -- plugging in the lamp, flipping the light switch. A channel, or energy worker, turns the switch for Spirit to flow into the situation.

3. Receiver Sometimes, such as when you are doing energy work on yourself, the receiver is awaiting the flow of Spirit. At other times, the receiver may be unaware but still accept the blessing. I do energy work on my dogs all the time, and while they may not understand what I'm doing, they certainly experience the results.

When and Where Can You Do Energy Work?

It's best to do it when and where you are least distracted, but if necessary, it can be done at anytime, anywhere you feel comfortable. I was at a high school football game once and sent healing to an injured player. At first it can help to practice it during meditation or in a peaceful, quiet setting to help you develop your practice uninterrupted.

What If A Healing Doesn't "Work?"

Usually there is one of two reasons why an energy session does not manifest the intended goal:

1. The receiver may block it. Either consciously or unconsciously, the receiver may not want to receive the healing energy. There can be very good reasons for this. I had the privilege of participating in a group healing for a woman who had been in a car accident. She was very conflicted because, while she wanted to feel better, a spontaneous healing might mean that her insurance would not cover all of the expenses she had incurred as a result of the accident. Several of us present could feel her resistance. Someone even said, "I felt like I was sending energy to a brick wall." While she did receive benefit from the work in that she walked away feeling calmer and more peaceful, she held onto the physical manifestations that she needed for her insurance claim.

There are those, too, who doubt your 'ability' to facilitate healing and are thus determined to prove that you cannot help them. Guess what. They will get what they want, even if it is to their own detriment. Whenever I offer to do energy work, I ask the potential recipient, "Are you open to the possibility that this will (*insert healing intention, such as* remove your growth, relieve your rash, etc.)?" If they are not open to it, I ask if they want to become willing to receive it. Spirit can use any opening, no matter how miniscule.

2. A karmic agreement may prevent it. There can also be a previous agreement with Spirit that overrides the work, such as the recipient chose this experience before coming into this incarnation. I knew a very spiritual woman who had cancer and fought it with great tenacity. She publicly affirmed on many occasions that she would be healed. Unfortunately, she died less than a year later.

I believe she had an agreement with Spirit even before she started this human journey, that it would be complete when it was. In other words, she had already determined that she would die from it before she even got sick, and no amount of healing efforts could reverse that decision.

We are not in charge here on earth, a power greater than us is. While we can use the power for many good things, sometimes the highest good is something other than what we might imagine it to be. However, no energy work ever occurs without a blessing for someone somehow. The "healer" always benefits in the action of doing good for someone else; and usually there are collateral blessings as well, such as something so small as a good night's sleep for everyone involved.

What Is Reiki?

Reiki (pronounced ray-key) is a form of energy work that involves the learning of symbols to assist with the healing and receiving three different levels of attunements. It is believed that Jesus and many other historical healers practiced Reiki. Those who receive Reiki attunements say that they can feel a heightened sense of energy moving through them with each new level. It continues to amaze me when I see the effects of Reiki.

While there is some confusion between a Reiki attunement and a Reiki treatment, let me explain how I use the terms. When a person comes to me for Reiki, what they receive is a treatment, where I allow the energy to flow through me to them utilizing my Reiki training and the traditional symbols. Whenever I use Reiki for healing, I am giving a Reiki treatment. When I teach one of the levels of Reiki so that my client may become a certified practitioner – Reiki I, Reiki II, or Reiki Master – that is an attunement.

One of my most profound examples of Reiki's power, used along with the power of prayer, happened when my husband fell about 35 feet while painting our house. As soon as he was quiet on the ground, I instinctively placed my hands on him, one on his shoulder and the other on his right side. As soon as I touched him he moaned, "Ow! That's right where it hurts!" Momentarily appreciating Spirit's confirmation, I eased the pressure but kept my hand where it was. I called upon Spirit and visualized healing energy flowing into him where he needed it. I stayed in that position until the ambulance arrived and the paramedics asked me to move.

Later in the ER, the doctor finally came out to discuss the results of the CAT scan. He showed me where, "he almost tore off the bottom third of his liver." He gave me a puzzled look as he pointed to a dark line on the scan. "What I don't understand is there was very little bleeding. The liver is an organ that is full of blood, yet you can see there is not very much blood in his abdomen." I later remembered giving him Reiki and credit that for slowing the bleeding, paving the way for a full recovery.

There truly are no limits to the miracles that Spirit can accomplish in your life. The paths are myriad -- whether it's a keenly tuned intuition, the ability to use Divine Energy for healing, or countless other spiritual outlets – and the Source is inside of you. In fact, your truest essence, the very center of your being is One with the Infinite. And you don't have to do a thing to earn it. It's been there all along!

In A Nutshell

Recently I learned that brain research supports one of my three agreements that I have with Spirit. I found that after a session was over I couldn't remember details that I told clients. I decided to give myself permission to allow the information uncovered during a reading to walk out the door with the client and not hold myself responsible for remembering what was said. Turns out, the reason I have trouble remembering is because that part of my brain is quiet while I am communicating with Spirit and my "rememberer" is not engaged. In my other two agreements, I have asked Spirit not to tell me anything I must hold back from a client, and to give me only the information my clients need.

I also discussed karma, energy that seems to continue from one lifetime to the next, how to identify karmic ties with people, and ways to deal with it. The next topic was chakras, energy centers at different points in the body represented by certain colors. I connected the emotional centers covered in Chapter 5 with the chakra points to help you better understand yourself and others.

The final discussion was energy work. Whenever people allow divine energy to flow through, they are doing energy work. Divine energy is ever present, and simply asking it to flow through you creates the connection that you need. Ultimately, there is a greater power in force that can create healing or remove energy blockages, and sometimes it is not in divine order for the healing to take place. Reiki is just one of many types of energy work in practice today. And it is true with all types of energy work that it is "all about the intention."

Chapter Ten Exercises

1. Think about your relationship with your Higher Power, your Spirit Guides. Can you think of any agreements you might have, or want to have? Jot them down.

_____

_____

2. With whom in your life (living or deceased) do you know you "have karma?" Can you describe feeling at home with (or repelled by) someone for no reason?

_____

_____

3. Focus your thoughts on each chakra, one at a time, and see if you can get a sense of them, where they are and what the energy feels like. Notice if you feel a heaviness or lightness in any of them. Practice associating the colors with the location of each chakra.

4. Most of us have some residual energy in all of our emotional centers. First see if you are experiencing discomfort or pain anywhere in your body, and identify what feeling is associated with the body part. Now fill out the following:

I am angry about_____

I am sad about _____

I am afraid of _____

I am ashamed of _____

Notice how when you think about (and then experience) emotions you can feel them in various parts of your body.

5. The most basic form of energy work is visualization -- picturing someone healthy or healed. Think of someone you know who is ill. Get a vivid image of them in your mind and then imagine what they will look like once they are well. See them vibrant and alive, happy and joyful. Describe how it will look and feel once they are restored to perfect health.

_____

_____

6. Now imagine how it would feel if your heart's desire manifested in this moment. Describe your heart's desire(s):

_____

_____

7. How would it feel to experience it actually happening?

_____

_____

11
Smooth Sailing

Writing this last chapter brings up some bittersweet memories of when my children would return to school after summer vacation. While I was proud that they were moving up to a new level (or a new school), I had a hard time letting go. I grieved their moving away from me. The same is true of you, my dear readers. In much the same way that I transitioned from automatic writing to verbal readings so I could cram as much information into the allotted time, so it is with this last chapter. I want to make sure I have given you plenty to work with and to whisper, "look both ways before crossing the street" in your ear one more time. Thus, this chapter has taken me the longest to put down on "paper."

Meditation

While there are many suggestions already given, I saved meditation for last. Its benefits would fill volumes, so I'll cut to the chase. An hour of meditation is said to be as restorative to your body as one and a half hours of sleep. It lowers stress as well as blood pressure; has been known to have positive effects on your outlook and peace of mind.

When the first psychic told me that I had intuitive ability, I asked her what I needed to do to get it started. "Meditation," she answered. At the time I was working full-time with a toddler and whenever I had a quiet moment and shut my eyes, sleep soon followed.

However, I made some attempts and recalled the first time I tried meditation as a senior in high school. I was given the assignment to read an article in a psychology magazine on meditation and report on it to the class. We were each given a different article and I marvel at how perfect that one turned out to be for me later in life. After reading about meditation and its myriad benefits to body, mind, and soul, I decided that I needed to try it, although admittedly it scared me. I'm not sure what scared me, probably the anticipated loss of control, even though the article made it clear that one remains in contact with their conscious mind at all times. Honestly, I was afraid I would "go away and never come back!" Nevertheless, I proceeded.

I stretched out on my bed in the middle of the afternoon and decided I would meditate for ten minutes. A glance at the clock told me it was 4:23. While I cannot remember what techniques I used, I can tell you when my eyes opened it was 4:33. That in itself amazed me and lessened my fear although I didn't pick up the practice again until years later.

What Is Meditation?

There are as many answers to this question as there are people who meditate. The key indicator seems to be your brain. As I understand it, your brain has basically three wave states: awake, asleep, and meditation. When your brain is in the meditative state, I believe you have access to Spirit in a dimension not available in the other two states. The proof really is in the doing. I could prattle on and on about it, but one experience of it will give you all you need to know. There are experts who analyze how and why it works, and if this interests you, I encourage you to read further on the subject. For our purposes, let's just say that while you are in the relaxed state of meditation, your mind will accept the concept of your Oneness With All That Is more readily than while awake.

While I agree that walking can be meditative, if done in a mindful state, as can be washing the dishes or taking out the trash, the most beneficial practice seems to revolve around stillness and quiet. If you are using your walking times to talk to Spirit, please don't discontinue the practice, just consider adding some still, quiet times to your practice as well.

Why Meditate?

With a regular meditation practice in your life, you will find more...

> * Peace
> * Prosperity
> * Stillness
> * Bliss
> * Self-awareness
> * Relaxation
> * Grounding
> * Clarity/understanding

What *in You* Might Stand in Your Way?

I encourage you, just as you processed the obstacles in the first two chapters, to examine the following and see which ones apply to you.

* Believing you can't
* Fidgeting
* Interruption
* Feeling unworthy
* Trying too hard
* Preoccupation
* Racing thoughts
* Resistance
* Old belief patterns

Now don't beat yourself up if you see yourself in every one of them! The list is meant as information, not indictment. You can do this. Every item on the list applied (OK, still applies sometimes!) to me at one time or another. It is important to know what stands in your way in order to figure out how to get past it.

How Can You Get Past Your Obstacles?

1. Change your mind. Believe that you can. Know that you deserve to have a wonderful experience. You choose your thoughts. Choose quiet, peaceful ones.
2. Practice letting go and forgive yourself for your shortcomings, real or imagined.
3. Release pent-up energy. Dance, jog, do exercises, wear yourself out first! Stretch.
4. Visualize putting all your worries into a jar, closing the lid and setting it aside.
5. Allow yourself time for learning. You probably weren't successful the first time you tried to tie your shoe, yet you do so now without thinking.
6. Practice focusing your mind on just one thing at a time, even if for just a minute. Then extend the time each day.

How to Set the Stage for Meditation

Our bodies and minds respond to cues outside of ourselves, so when it's time to meditate put lots of them around. **Above all, make sure you are comfortable.**

1. Find a cozy place to sit. Maybe have a soft pillow or quilt nearby.
2. Make sure your clothes aren't too tight or stiff.
3. Ensure that the room is a comfortable temperature.
4. Surround yourself with things that suggest peace & quiet.
5. Soft lighting is good, even total darkness if you prefer.
6. An image of serenity can help get you started, such as a picture of a mountain stream or a lovely sunset.
7. Plan for quiet time when you won't be interrupted.
8. Turn the phone off (silent, not 'vibrate').
9. Play calming music; consider music that doesn't have a definite beat or rhythm.
10. Use aromatherapy. Burn a fragrant, soothing candle or incense.
11. Try to practice at a regular time to "set up your appointment with Spirit"

Techniques to Use During Meditation

As you develop your meditation practice, you may want to try different techniques.

1. Take a deep breath and relax your body.
2. State your intention to meditate.
3. Get into your "safe space:" Get quiet, peaceful.
4. See the White Light around you.
5. Validate yourself. Trust God.

6. Sit quietly and practice mindfulness. Observe your mood and your mind.
7. Use whatever imagery speaks to you such as:
    a. Imaging a golden light radiating above your head
    b. Picturing one of your Spirit guides or guardian angels
    c. Seeing yourself in your "special place"
8. Ask for what you want.
9. Be careful not to judge or edit if information comes to you. Be a neutral observer.
10. Allow yourself to stay in the meditative state as long as you are comfortable.
11. Bring yourself back to the present slowly: wiggling fingers, toes, stretching, etc.

A Suggested Meditation Script

You may want to record yourself reading this out loud to listen to on your audio player (digital, CD, or tape) while you practice meditation. It is in two parts: (1) relaxing the body and (2) shifting your mind.

Relaxing the Body

Allow your body to relax deeply, with each breath letting go of stress and tension. Feel yourself sinking into a blissful state. Imagine a beam of energy, pure love essence, emitting from the very center of the earth. Rising up through all the layers of the earth and entering into the soles of your feet. As you feel this pure love energy entering into your feet, notice how they relax and begin to feel heavy. Allow the energy to move through your feet – your toes, the balls and heels, tops and bottoms – to your ankles. Throughout your meditation time, your body will become more and more deeply relaxed and peaceful. Feel the energy move through your ankles into your lower legs – your calves and shins; then through your lower legs into your knees. When you allow your knees to relax, it is as though you are telling your body, "Go ahead and settle in, we won't be going anywhere for a while." You may or may not notice a few things that are happening inside your body by this time:

1. Your heart rate is slowing down, just a little.
2. Your breathing is also slowing down and getting a bit deeper.
3. Your brain is shifting to the brain wave of meditation. As soon as you first thought about doing this meditation, your brain began to ready itself for this shift, which it does easily, with no effort on your part.

Now notice the relaxation moving up your legs into your thighs. Some of our largest muscles are located in the upper legs, so when they relax, your entire body becomes that much more peaceful. As the energy continues to move up your body, feel it moving into your lower back, tailbone, pelvic floor, and lower torso. Imagine the pure energy soaking into the base of your spine, telling all your nerve endings to take a break. Moving up your body, through your pelvis, picture the love essence rising one vertebra at a time, sending out a message to all the parts of your body connected to those nerves, "All is well. Relax."

As the energy moves through your torso, notice how every muscle, tendon, ligament, organ – everything – at the corresponding level becomes relaxed and peaceful. At the same time, notice the pure love essence seeping into the tips of your fingers and thumbs, moving up into your hands, wrists, and arms. Imagine it moving up your body, creating this deep wave of relaxation that comes together at your shoulders. Our shoulders represent where we carry our responsibilities, so as the relaxing energy reaches your shoulders picture them becoming rounded on top. All of your responsibilities just slide off into a little pile on the floor next to you. You can pick them back up when you are finished, but for now let them go.

As the peace reaches your throat, you may notice your shoulders sinking down and your neck seeming to grow a little longer. Pay particular attention when the wave reaches your atlas, the last vertebra where your spinal column meets your skull. It is full of nerve endings and when you allow that pure love energy to sink in, your entire body reaches a much deeper state of calm. Continue sinking in while the wave moves through your head, feeling your jaw, mouth, nose, and the rest of your face losing expression until the pure energy reaches your crown.

Now take a few moments to enjoy how wonderful it feels when your entire body is relaxed and peaceful. We can go for long periods of time without completely relaxing our bodies; even during sleep we can remain tense. *So, this luxurious feeling of complete serenity is something to savor.*

Shifting Your Mind

Much is written about 'where' the spirit connects to the body and while I believe our human bodies are intimately connected to our spiritual bodies in every cell, there does seem to be some significance about the crown of the head, as though our spiritual selves continue beyond the top of the head. Whether this is factual or not, I suggest you try something that was taught to me in high school English class -- "willing suspension of disbelief." Let go of your doubts and bear with me. Give this concept a try and see if it works for you.

So imagine that not only does your spiritual self extend beyond you, it is centered in a ball of white light concentrated about a foot or two above your scalp. Bring all of your consciousness up to that ball of light. Take as long as you need and make it a drifting, easy process rather than a forceful one. Land softly in the light and look all around you. Marvel at how beautiful the light is, how it dances and moves, how it shimmers and glows, how it seems to be moving in every direction. In fact, when you take notice, it appears to be going right *through* you! On closer observation, you can see that you *are* light. You are One with the light!

Notice the feelings:
- Total peace
- Complete acceptance
- Unconditional love
- Joy
- Euphoria
- Bliss
- A certainty that all is well

Spend as much time as you like experiencing your spiritual self and when you are ready, gently bring your consciousness back to your body. Reorient yourself to time and place, wiggle your fingers and toes, stretch, and then open your eyes.

Other Meditation Techniques

There are many other techniques you can use to practice meditation. I recommend that you use the Relaxing the Body practice at the beginning of each session. It is always beneficial to allow our human forms the chance to release stress and tension.

Visualization is one of my favorites, where you create images in your mind. You can use it to discern additional intuitive information, set the course for your life, or gain understanding about situations in your life. It is like setting your creative mind out to play! You never know what you are going to come up with.

To intuit information, create a scene in your mind and then allow your imagination (Spirit) to complete the picture. For example, if you are wondering which car would be best for you to purchase, imagine you are walking into your garage and see what is parked there. Or visualize yourself driving the car off the sales lot and notice what it looks like. Keep creating different scenarios until you feel you have gotten the information you seek.

To set the course for your life, picture yourself doing what you *love*. Create images in your mind for what your ideal day looks like, your best living spaces, your wonderful relationships, the balance in your bank account, the fantastic trips you are going to take. Spirit is infinite, as are the possibilities for joy in your life. Do not try to figure out the 'how,' just picture the scene once you have arrived. Spirit will chart the best course for you, so spend some time in visualization to get clear on what you want. (You can always add to your prayer, "this or something better.") Visualizing *what* you want is your way of showing Spirit in which direction you would like to venture. I promise you, God's idea of *how* to get there will be *way* more fun than even anything you can cook up!

Using meditation to gain understanding about situations in your life can take many avenues. You may ask Spirit to show you the situation from a different perspective, such as how it looks to the others involved. This could allow you to see that while you are acting out of a certain set of expectations, your actions are perceived quite differently than you intend. Or, you might ask Spirit to show you possible outcomes. One technique I use in readings, that could also be helpful in meditation, is to present Spirit with the potential paths that could be taken and ask for a glimpse "down the road." Observe not only what is revealed but also how it feels and how much light or color is around the options. I suggest you also create a path called the Road Not Yet Considered, to allow Spirit the opportunity to show you even more possibilities than the ones you have thought of so far.

Symbolism is often used during meditation, as it is in readings, dreams, and other intuitive endeavors. If you are confused about what a symbol means, I suggest that you describe it out loud, either to yourself or a trusted friend. It is amazing how much we can learn by our own descriptions of things. For example, you might be a college student and dream that you went to class and your classroom was flooding with water and you could barely keep your head above the surface. Upon describing this aloud, you could hear yourself saying that you feel like you are "in over your head" in that class, something you may have not wanted to consciously admit to yourself. The meanings of symbols are bound only by your imagination, and you get to decide the significance and interpretation of things created by your own subconscious.

Playful Meditations are something I truly hope that you allow yourself to explore. For example, you can imagine yourself coming to a temple where a message is written for you on a book on the marble pedestal. Or you can go to "the most peaceful place on earth" and see where your subconscious brings you. You can imagine that Spirit has given you a gift and then observe what shows up for you during your meditation and how it will help you. I once participated in a meditation led by another psychic in Sedona who used this technique. My gift was a beautiful crystal pendant. Upon closer observation, I could see that it was a quartz crystal that I already had in my possession. A few months later I created the pendant for myself and treasure it very much. It reminds me of the meditation and the wonderful synchronicity I experienced during that trip.

I was leading a regular group meditation in my home a few years ago. One evening instead of our usual deep, serious session, I decided it was time we had a little fun. I'll share the basics of the meditation as best I can recall and invite you to create your own version or repeat it just as we did it. After doing the Body Relaxation, here is what I told the group:

Thought Garden Meditation

We are going to visit the garden where we plant, grow, and cultivate our thoughts. You may believe that your thoughts are mainly positive and results-oriented, or even suspect that they are mostly fear-based. Let's visit the garden where our thoughts are growing and see for ourselves. First picture the location of your garden. Lush meadow? Mountain valley? Dry desert? Allow yourself to simply observe as you view the vista surrounding your garden. Now approach your garden and notice. Is it fenced in or open? Is the fence a stone wall, wood picket, barbed wire or something else?

There will be four areas inside your garden plus another in the center we will visit. The first area represents your thoughts on your life work or career. Go to the Work section and look around. What is growing here if anything -- annuals (that last only a season) or perennials (that come back year after year)? Trees? Bushes? Look carefully as you proceed through each section of your garden and notice how it feels.

Proceed to the second area, which is where you grow your thoughts on your Relationships. Notice what is growing here, if you have any statuary or a bench perhaps. How does it feel? Are there lots of things alive and well here or just a few? How lush is this area of your garden?

Now move on to the third area, which is about Children. It can represent your own inner child or the children in your life. Notice how much attention you have paid to this area and, again, what is growing here. What colors do you see? Make as many observations as you like.

Located nearby is the fourth section, which is about Play and Fun. How much energy have you put into this part of your garden? Is it thriving or somewhat neglected? Are there any amusing decorations? Is it a happy place? Have you watered this area of your garden lately?

Now in the very center of your garden is your Bonus Area. It can be anything you want it to be. Allow yourself to know what is represented here and what information you can ascertain to help you in your day-to-day life. Maybe there is a plaque here with a message for you. Is there a windmill or a well?

Before you leave the Garden of your Thoughts, there is one more thing to see. Just above your garden is your very own Monument of Intentions. This symbolizes how you set intentions for your life, what they are, and how they are manifesting for you. What does it look like? Are there any symbols on it, any writing? What is it made of? What is its size? When you are finished visiting your garden, allow yourself to come back to the present moment.

Symbols in this meditation

Most of the symbols you have witnessed in this meditation will be obvious to you. Allow yourself to accept whatever has been revealed as information that may be helpful going forward. Please don't feel badly if you witnessed something you did not like, and don't place too much emphasis on any one thing. Your overall impression, however, could be very valuable.

In meditation or through your own intuition, when you encounter symbols, or animals for example, that seem indecipherable to you, I suggest you do an Internet search. A few years ago, I repeatedly encountered owls over a week's period, while on my morning walk through my neighborhood and in the evening while at home, I both heard them calling and saw them fly right overhead. It sparked my curiosity so I searched "owl totem," hoping to find the Native American meaning for when someone considers an owl to be his or her totem (or spirit) animal. What I discovered delighted me. The owl is considered the totem animal of a psychic! It surprises me that I hadn't seen them sooner. I am not suggesting that every Internet search will produce helpful information, but it doesn't hurt to try.

I sincerely suggest that you give meditation a chance. It has the potential to benefit you in countless ways, and once you master the technique, it is practically effortless.

Developing Your Intuition Is a Process

Please be kind to yourself and do not expect yourself to develop keenly accurate psychic senses overnight. While my transition into doing automatic writing did pretty much happen in a couple of evenings, the intuitive abilities that I have now developed over decades. And they are still far from perfect. Once I admit to myself that I am not in charge, and that I have no control over what information is given to me or how much detail comes through, I can be at peace with it. I am open to becoming a more open channel of God's good in this world, in whatever form it may take: offering insight, providing comfort, or simply being kind and loving. *When I am open, I am teachable.* One of my favorite sayings is, "God can't steer a parked car." So I try to get moving and create openings for Spirit to work in my life.

Reading for Loved Ones

I am often asked if I do psychic readings for myself or those closest to me, and the short answer is no. It is difficult for me to discern the difference between my insight and my will when I am greatly invested in the information or the outcome. So I do not use my typical technique of sitting down at my reading table and allowing Spirit to communicate with me; but I do use other methods instead. Automatic or channeled writing is one way I can divine answers for loved ones or myself. For some reason, I am able to detach myself from the message when I am channeling with a pen in hand.

I also use tarot cards and other divination tools. When a certain card appears in a reading, I know that I did not deliberately select it (because it was face-down!), that it showed up through an energy outside of me. There are many tools available today; I would encourage you to trust your instincts in choosing those that are right for you. I have used a pendulum in the past, but find that it is too slow of a process for me. Once you begin to trust yourself, Spirit will find many ways to communicate with and through you.

That said, I feel honor-bound to mention one of my children's favorite games, "Let's Get Mom to Predict." Living 600+ miles from our extended family has resulted in many, many long drives, with lots of hours to fill. One of my clever offspring figured out that when Mom is sufficiently distracted by driving (but not in heavy traffic) she can suspend her disbelief and come up with some pretty accurate insights into the futures of various family members. While I come up with the information, my shotgun rider takes notes. I would say my accuracy is not as high as normal during these 'sessions,' but they take what they can get! One summer I predicted that my oldest daughter would have a wonderful school year coming up. I saw her having a close boyfriend for the better part of the year, and saw the two of them practically inseparable. "But," I cautioned her, "I see your best friend getting sick at the beginning of the year and missing a lot of school. I'd guess she has mono." Well the descriptions were quite accurate, only I had the two girls mixed up. It was my daughter who got sick and her friend who got the boyfriend!

An interesting note about "Let's Get Mom to Predict," is that the scribe does not always write down exactly what I say. When I go back to read the notes, I am intrigued at how my words are sometimes translated to mean things I did not express. The irony we have discovered is that what is written down can be more accurate than the actual words I spoke. Spirit, it appears, works through the entire process, not only providing me with insights and visions, but also providing my scribe the best way to write down the messages.

Which brings me to my final point, one that I have expressed in various ways throughout the book but which bears repeating one last time.

God Is In Charge

I have a friend who often, when faced with a decision, will say, "I don't know, let me contact Headquarters." Headquarters was her symbol for the force in charge, God, Spirit, Universal Life Force, the 'powers that be.' Part of my concept of God is an energy field that permeates all matter, always aligned with the highest good of the individual and the group as a whole. Similar to the current in a river, if you let go it will take you where you need to go, but you can fight it and try to swim upstream if you want. Ultimately, the current is always the best way to go, and the easiest.

This may seem to contradict my earlier discussion about your choosing the 'what' and God figuring out the 'how.' I believe that our heart's desires and our dreams come from God, which we discover when we tune in to the best version of ourselves and allow our own goodness to bubble up. I am talking about the major decisions we make about the courses our lives will take. Our free will gives us the leeway to settle for mediocre instead of our highest, most wonderful possibility. But when we focus on Spirit, check in with Headquarters on a regular basis, wonderful things happen in and around us. And the balance leans more and more toward joy and happiness.

May you find joy in your life,
In yourself,
And in those around you
Namaste.

Chapter Eleven Exercises

1. Try to meditate. Use any of the techniques mentioned in the chapter. What were your impressions? Were they different when you tried different techniques?

_____

_____

_____

2. Think of a recent dream you had. What were the symbols in the dream? Did you know upon waking what they meant?

_____

_____

3. Practice the Thought Garden meditation. What did your garden look like? Describe each of the four areas: work, relationships, children, and fun. Feel free to change the areas to suit you.

_____

_____

_____

_____

4. What was in your bonus area? Describe your Monument of Intentions.

_____

5. Try reading for a friend or loved one and allow them to take notes. Notice the differences between what you said and what was written.

_____

_____

_____

_____

6. What do you want from your life? Write it down.

_____

_____

_____

_____

_____

_____

Now go live it! ☺

Acknowledgements

The words Thank You cannot encompass my gratitude for the support, love and encouragement I have received. Let me apologize in advance if I have forgotten anyone. My journey has been immeasurably aided, centering on my precious husband, Lance, who gave me the space to create and the push by asking, "So when are you going to write your book?" Starting with my parents Betty and Don, and including the siblings who alternately harassed and (mostly) loved me from childhood —Beth, Don, and Brent— then the three who made me a mom and gave me so many stories —Tara, Stacey, and Hayley— adding the two who made me a stepmom —Brett and Chase— and including in order of appearance Gary, Ken, Mindy, Laura, Jerry, Jared, Kara, Ryan, Mallary, and Lacy— my family is the heart of my life and my psychic development. They create my foundation and my happiness.

This book would not be what it is without the help of Editor/Friend Extraordinaire Julie. Her kind words and thorough but gentle editing offered needed perspective—and touched me deeply. Final proofing and supremely encouraging words from my Partners-in-Crime Tam & Beth (and Tara, Stacey, and Hayley) gave the finishing touches and much loving support. My early efforts were well received by friends and family—you know who you are—and I greatly value you. I must credit the visual appearance to my precious son-in-law, Ryan Dale. He patiently walked me through the design process, offering excellent suggestions and ultimately completing the beautiful cover design as well as the interior set up.

I must also mention those who helped me develop skills in the two areas most needed for this book: writing and intuition. My writing ability is a credit to Sr. Andrea, who laid down the law and established the foundation for my love of the written word and who still inspires me today, and Sr. Teresa who taught, "Words are your friends." Dr. Larry Lain and Dr. Kath Williams prodded me into becoming a professional writer, and then later supported my "new career." As I grew into being a psychic, those early clients who kept coming back—especially Charles, the 'fella in the jeep'—helped me believe I had something to offer. My students and clients have each played a unique role, notably those who have taken my classes, had private sessions, attended my meditations, and repeatedly inquired about this work.

It is my deepest hope that I have enhanced the lives of those mentioned above and my readers, and that my efforts will be received in the spirit they are intended—to be a blessing and a joy. Truly, I love each one of you.

About the Author

Debra Busemeyer Baker has been helping people transform their lives since 1988 when she discovered she had the ability to do automatic writing and communicate with angels, spirit guides, and people who have died. Now she is a gifted psychic medium, Reiki Master, crystal and energy worker, and Oneness Blessing Giver. Her readings have been described as "life changing," "profound," and "extremely accurate." She teaches classes and leads meditations through a variety of venues in the Kansas City area where she resides with her husband, Lance, a smattering of ghosts and spirits, and a beagle named Gus.

Contact Information

Debra is available for speaking engagements, group sessions, and private appointment. She may be reached at:

Email: amazing.intuition.book@gmail.com
Facebook page: Healing Debra
Website: http://htransformations.tripod.com

CPSIA information can be obtained
at www.ICGtesting.com
Printed in the USA
FFOW03n1618230614

6038FF